Clean Code: An Agile Guide to Software Craft

Kameron Hussain and Frahaan Hussain

Published by Sonar Publishing, 2023.

While every precaution has been taken in the preparation of this book, the publisher assumes no responsibility for errors or omissions, or for damages resulting from the use of the information contained herein.

CLEAN CODE: AN AGILE GUIDE TO SOFTWARE CRAFT

First edition. October 15, 2023.

Copyright © 2023 Kameron Hussain and Frahaan Hussain.

ISBN: 979-8223565338

Written by Kameron Hussain and Frahaan Hussain.

Table of Contents

1. Large and Complex Methods

2. Lack of Modularity

3. Inconsistent Naming

4. Low Testability

5. Inefficient Data Structures

Section 16.3: The Refactoring Process

1. Create a Test Suite

2. Identify and Isolate Concerns

3. Extract Small, Focused Functions

4. Improve Naming and Documentation

5. Enhance Testability

6. Replace Inefficient Data Structures and Algorithms

7. Continuous Testing and Validation

8. Incremental Refactoring

9. Code Review and Collaboration

10. Measure Progress

Section 16.4: Incremental Refactoring Steps

Step 1: Create a Test Suite

Step 2: Isolate Parsing Logic

Step 3: Refactor Date Calculation Methods

Step 4: Improve Naming and Documentation

Step 5: Extract Formatting Logic

Step 6: Enhance Testability

Step 7: Replace Inefficient Algorithms

Step 8: Continuous Testing and Validation

Step 9: Incremental and Iterative

Step 10: Code Review and Collaboration

Step 11: Measure Progress

Section 16.5: The Benefits of Clean Code

1. Improved Readability

2. Enhanced Maintainability

3. Reduced Technical Debt

4. Easier Collaboration

5. Better Debugging

6. Increased Developer Productivity

7. Code Reusability

8. Confidence in Changes

9. Enhanced Documentation

10. Long-Term Cost Savings

11. Developer Satisfaction

Chapter 1: Clean Code

1.1 What Is Clean Code?

Clean code is the foundation of high-quality software development. It encompasses the practice of writing code that is not only functional but also easy to read, understand, and maintain. Clean code is like a well-organized and well-documented piece of literature that can be comprehended by anyone who reads it. It strives to minimize complexity, eliminate ambiguity, and follow established coding conventions and best practices.

In the world of software development, clean code is often equated with code that exhibits clarity, simplicity, and elegance. Clean code is not a rigid set of rules but rather a set of principles and guidelines that help developers create software that is efficient, bug-free, and a pleasure to work with.

The Benefits of Clean Code

Clean code offers several advantages to developers and organizations:

1. **Readability**: Clean code is easy to read and understand, reducing the time required for developers to grasp its functionality. This leads to faster development and maintenance.
2. **Maintainability**: Code that follows clean code principles is easier to maintain over time. Bugs can be quickly identified and fixed, and new features can be added with minimal disruption.
3. **Collaboration**: Clean code promotes collaboration among team members. When everyone can understand the code

easily, collaboration becomes smoother and more efficient.

4. **Reduced Technical Debt**: Technical debt refers to the long-term costs of maintaining poorly written code. Clean code minimizes technical debt by ensuring that code is of high quality from the start.

5. **Improved Testing**: Clean code is easier to test, leading to more thorough and effective testing procedures. This, in turn, results in more reliable software.

6. **Enhanced Debugging**: Debugging clean code is less challenging because it is well-organized and logically structured.

Characteristics of Clean Code

Clean code exhibits several key characteristics:

• **Consistency**: Clean code adheres to consistent coding conventions and formatting standards throughout the project.

• **Clarity**: Clean code uses meaningful and descriptive names for variables, functions, and classes. It avoids cryptic abbreviations or overly short identifiers.

• **Simplicity**: Clean code is free from unnecessary complexity. It follows the KISS (Keep It Simple, Stupid) principle.

• **Modularity**: Clean code is organized into well-defined modules or functions, each responsible for a specific task. This promotes reusability and maintainability.

- **Minimal Dependencies**: Clean code minimizes dependencies between modules, reducing the risk of ripple effects when making changes.

- **Testability**: Clean code is designed with testing in mind, making it easier to write unit tests and ensure software reliability.

In summary, clean code is the cornerstone of effective software development. It not only benefits developers but also contributes to the overall success of software projects by enhancing readability, maintainability, and collaboration while reducing technical debt and the likelihood of defects. As we delve deeper into this book, we will explore the principles and practices that lead to clean code and discuss how they can be applied in real-world software development scenarios.

1.2 Why Does Clean Code Matter?

Clean code matters significantly in the world of software development for several compelling reasons. It is not merely an abstract concept or a matter of personal preference; it has tangible and far-reaching impacts on the quality, maintainability, and success of software projects. In this section, we will explore the key reasons why clean code is of paramount importance.

1.2.1 Readability and Understanding

One of the primary reasons clean code is crucial is its impact on readability and understanding. Code is not just meant for machines; it is also meant to be read and understood by humans. In a collaborative development environment, multiple developers may work on the same codebase. Clean code ensures that the logic and intentions behind the code are easily discernible, reducing the cognitive load on developers trying to understand it. This leads to faster onboarding of new team members and efficient collaboration.

Consider the following example:

 # Unclean Code

a = b + c - d * e

In this unclean code snippet, it is not immediately clear what the code is doing. Are we performing mathematical operations, or is there some specific logic behind it? In contrast, clean code would use meaningful variable names and possibly break down the operations into smaller, well-named functions, making the code's purpose clear:

 # Clean Code

result = calculate_total_price(base_price, tax_rate, discount_percentage)

In clean code, it is evident that we are calculating the total price, and the function's name and parameters provide additional context.

1.2.2 Maintainability

Maintaining software over time is a significant part of the development process. Clean code is easier to maintain because it follows established coding conventions and best practices. When you need to make changes or fix bugs, you can do so with confidence, knowing that clean code is less prone to unintended side effects. Additionally, clean code encourages the practice of refactoring, which involves improving the code's structure without changing its functionality. This helps keep the codebase healthy and adaptable.

1.2.3 Debugging and Error Detection

Clean code simplifies the debugging process. When code is well-organized and adheres to clean code principles, it is easier to isolate issues, identify their causes, and fix them. Clean code also promotes the use of meaningful variable and function names, which can provide clues about the purpose of different code segments. This speeds up the debugging process and reduces the time and effort required to find and resolve errors.

1.2.4 Collaboration

In a collaborative software development environment, multiple developers, designers, and stakeholders may work together on a project. Clean code acts as a common language that facilitates communication among team members. When everyone can understand the code easily, collaboration becomes more efficient, and there is less room for misunderstandings or misinterpretations of the code's functionality. This leads to smoother project development and reduces the likelihood of costly mistakes.

1.2.5 Code Reviews and Quality Assurance

Code reviews are a fundamental part of maintaining code quality. Clean code makes code reviews more productive and effective. Reviewers can focus on higher-level aspects of the code, such as architecture and design, rather than getting bogged down in deciphering poorly written or convoluted code. Moreover, clean code aligns with quality assurance practices by reducing the likelihood of hidden defects and making it easier to write comprehensive tests.

1.2.6 Long-Term Sustainability

Software projects are not short-term endeavors; they often have long lifespans. Clean code contributes to the long-term sustainability of a project. It minimizes technical debt, which refers to the cumulative cost of postponing necessary work on the codebase. With clean code, it is easier to adapt to changing requirements, add new features, and address evolving business needs without the codebase becoming unwieldy and fragile.

In conclusion, clean code is not a matter of personal preference; it is a critical aspect of software development that impacts readability, maintainability, debugging, collaboration, code reviews, and long-term sustainability. It is an investment in the success of a software project and should be a fundamental practice for all software developers. The principles of clean code, which we will explore in this book, provide valuable guidance for achieving these benefits.

1.3 The Principles of Clean Code

Clean code is not a vague concept but rather a set of principles and guidelines that developers can follow to ensure that their code is of high quality and easy to maintain. These principles have been developed and refined over years of software engineering practice and are widely accepted as best practices in the industry. In this section, we will delve into some of the core principles of clean code.

1.3.1 DRY (Don't Repeat Yourself) Principle

The DRY principle is a fundamental tenet of clean code. It emphasizes the importance of avoiding code duplication. When the same code logic is repeated in multiple places within a codebase, it becomes challenging to maintain consistency and can lead to errors when changes are made. Instead, clean code encourages developers to write code once and reuse it where necessary.

Consider the following example:

 # Unclean Code

def calculate_area_of_rectangle(length, width):

return length * width

def calculate_area_of_square(side):

return side * side

In this unclean code, the calculation of area is repeated in two different functions, leading to code duplication. Clean code, following the DRY principle, would refactor this code to eliminate duplication:

 # Clean Code

def calculate_area(length, width):

return length * width

Now, there's a single function for calculating the area, and it can be used for both rectangles and squares.

1.3.2 SRP (Single Responsibility Principle)

The Single Responsibility Principle states that a function, method, or class should have a single reason to change. In other words, it should have one clear and well-defined responsibility. This principle encourages developers to break down complex tasks into smaller, more manageable components, each responsible for a specific aspect of the functionality.

For example, consider a class that handles both user authentication and database access. This class violates the SRP because it has two distinct responsibilities: managing user authentication and database interaction. Clean code adhering to the SRP would split these responsibilities into separate classes or functions, each with a single responsibility.

 # Unclean Code violating SRP

class AuthAndDatabaseManager:

def authenticate_user(self, username, password):

 # Authenticate user logic

def connect_to_database(self, host, username, password):

 # Database connection logic

def query_database(self, sql):

 # Database query logic

Clean code following the SRP would refactor this code into separate classes for authentication and database management.

1.3.3 KISS (Keep It Simple, Stupid) Principle

The KISS principle advocates simplicity in code design. Clean code should strive to be as simple as possible without sacrificing functionality. Complexity can introduce unnecessary confusion, increase the likelihood of errors, and make code more challenging to maintain.

The KISS principle suggests that developers should favor straightforward, clear, and easy-to-understand solutions over overly complex ones. It encourages the removal of unnecessary abstractions, conditional branches, and convoluted logic.

```python
# Unclean Code with unnecessary complexity

def calculate_discounted_price(base_price, is_member, has_coupon):

    if is_member:

        if has_coupon:

            return apply_member_discount(apply_coupon(base_price))

        else:

            return apply_member_discount(base_price)

    elif has_coupon:

        return apply_coupon(base_price)

    else:

        return base_price
```

Clean code following the KISS principle would simplify this code to improve readability and maintainability.

1.3.4 YAGNI (You Ain't Gonna Need It) Principle

The YAGNI principle advises against adding functionality or code that is not currently needed. It encourages developers to avoid speculative or premature optimizations and additions. The rationale is that adding unnecessary features or complexity can increase code fragility and make it more challenging to maintain.

Clean code adhering to the YAGNI principle focuses on addressing the immediate requirements and defers decisions about future functionality until they become necessary. This approach ensures that the code remains lean and relevant to the current project's needs.

In summary, these principles are fundamental to clean code and guide developers in creating code that is efficient, readable, maintainable, and adaptable. By following these principles, developers can improve the quality of their code and contribute to the overall success of software projects. Throughout this book, we will explore these principles in more depth and provide practical examples of how to apply them in real-world coding scenarios.

1.4 A Case for Software Craftsmanship

Software craftsmanship is a philosophy that aligns closely with the principles of clean code. It emphasizes the idea that writing code is not just a mechanical task but an art that requires skill, care, and dedication. In this section, we will make a case for software craftsmanship and explore how it relates to the creation of clean code.

1.4.1 Beyond Functional Code

While functional code that meets the project's requirements is essential, software craftsmanship takes it a step further. It recognizes that code should not only work but also be elegant, maintainable, and a joy to work with. A software craftsman or craftswoman strives to create code that is not just a means to an end but a work of art in its own right.

1.4.2 Code as a Reflection of Thought

Software is a manifestation of human thought and creativity. Code is the medium through which developers express their ideas and solutions. Software craftsmanship recognizes that well-written code is a reflection of clear thinking and careful problem-solving. Just as a well-crafted painting or sculpture reflects the artist's skill and vision, clean code reflects the developer's craftsmanship.

1.4.3 Continuous Improvement

Software craftsmanship is a commitment to continuous improvement. Craftsmen and craftswomen understand that there is always room for improvement in their work. They seek feedback, learn from their mistakes, and actively look for ways to enhance their coding skills. This dedication to improvement leads to the creation of increasingly better code over time.

1.4.4 Attention to Detail

Craftsmanship is often associated with attention to detail. In software development, this means paying close attention to every aspect of the code, from variable names to code organization. Clean code, with its emphasis on meaningful names and well-structured functions, is a manifestation of this attention to detail.

1.4.5 Code That Stands the Test of Time

Software craftsmanship is about building code that is durable and can withstand the test of time. It's not just about delivering a quick solution but about creating software that can evolve and adapt as requirements change. Clean code, with its focus on maintainability, plays a crucial role in achieving this longevity.

1.4.6 Pride in Work

Software craftsmanship instills a sense of pride in the work of developers. Craftsmen and craftswomen take pride in creating code that is not just functional but also beautiful and well-crafted. This sense of pride can be a powerful motivator and can lead to higher job satisfaction and greater job performance.

1.4.7 Collaboration and Mentorship

Craftsmanship is often a collaborative effort. Developers who embrace software craftsmanship are eager to collaborate with others, share knowledge, and mentor less experienced developers. This culture of collaboration and knowledge sharing contributes to the growth and improvement of the entire team.

1.4.8 Balancing Pragmatism and Perfection

While software craftsmanship values high-quality code, it also recognizes the need for pragmatism. Not every piece of code needs to be a masterpiece, and there are times when quick and dirty solutions are appropriate. However, craftsmen and craftswomen understand the difference between necessary pragmatism and lazy shortcuts that can lead to technical debt.

In conclusion, software craftsmanship is not just a buzzword but a mindset that promotes the creation of clean, high-quality code. It is a commitment to excellence in software development, an aspiration to create code that is both functional and beautiful. As we explore the principles of clean code in this book, keep in mind that clean code and software craftsmanship go hand in hand. By embracing both, developers can elevate their coding skills and contribute to the creation of exceptional software.

1.5 How Clean Code Enhances Agile Development

Clean code and agile development are two concepts that complement each other well. Agile development methodologies, such as Scrum and Kanban, emphasize flexibility, collaboration, and responsiveness to changing requirements. Clean code aligns perfectly with these principles and can greatly enhance the effectiveness of agile development practices. In this section, we will explore how clean code contributes to and enhances agile development.

1.5.1 Readability and Adaptability

In agile development, the ability to adapt to changing requirements is paramount. Clean code, with its emphasis on readability and simplicity, makes it easier for development teams to understand, modify, and extend code quickly. When requirements change, clean code can be more readily adapted to accommodate those changes without introducing unnecessary complexity or increasing the risk of defects.

1.5.2 Continuous Integration and Delivery

Agile development encourages continuous integration and delivery (CI/CD) practices, where code changes are integrated into the main codebase and delivered to users frequently. Clean code is essential for successful CI/CD because it reduces the likelihood of integration conflicts and makes it easier to perform automated testing. When code is clean, it is less likely to introduce bugs that could disrupt the CI/CD pipeline.

1.5.3 Collaboration and Code Reviews

Agile development promotes collaboration among team members, including developers, testers, designers, and product owners. Clean code fosters effective collaboration because it is easier to understand and discuss during code reviews and team discussions. Code reviews in agile teams become more productive when the code under review adheres to clean code principles, allowing team members to focus on higher-level design and functionality.

1.5.4 Test-Driven Development (TDD)

Test-driven development is a core practice in agile development, where tests are written before code is implemented. Clean code plays a crucial role in TDD by making it easier to write meaningful tests. Clean code is inherently more testable because it follows principles such as single responsibility and modularity, allowing individual components to be tested in isolation. This makes TDD more effective and efficient.

 # Example of clean code facilitating TDD

```
def            calculate_total_price(base_price,          tax_rate,
discount_percentage):
```

 # Calculate total price logic

In the clean code example above, it is straightforward to write unit tests to verify the calculate_total_price function's behavior.

1.5.5 Agile Refactoring

Agile development encourages regular refactoring of code to improve its structure and maintainability. Clean code makes refactoring easier and less risky. Developers can confidently refactor clean code because they can rely on meaningful variable and function names and a clear understanding of the code's purpose.

1.5.6 Reduced Technical Debt

Technical debt, the accumulation of shortcuts and compromises in code quality, can impede agile development progress. Clean code helps reduce technical debt by maintaining code quality from the start. In agile projects, addressing technical debt becomes more manageable because clean code is easier to refactor and improve.

1.5.7 Empowering Cross-Functional Teams

Agile development encourages cross-functional teams with members who have diverse skills and roles. Clean code empowers cross-functional teams by providing a shared language and understanding of the codebase. Team members can collaborate effectively, regardless of their specific roles, when the code follows clean code principles.

In summary, clean code and agile development are mutually reinforcing practices. Clean code enhances agile development by promoting readability, adaptability, collaboration, and testing. It enables development teams to respond to changing requirements, deliver high-quality software continuously, and maintain a sustainable pace of development. By embracing clean code principles, agile teams can achieve greater efficiency and effectiveness in delivering valuable software to their customers.

Chapter 2: Meaningful Names

2.1 The Importance of Good Names

Choosing meaningful and descriptive names for variables, functions, classes, and other elements in your code is one of the fundamental principles of clean code. Good names improve code readability, enhance understanding, and make maintenance easier. In this section, we'll explore the significance of good names in clean code and provide guidelines for effective naming.

2.1.1 Readability and Comprehensibility

Good names contribute significantly to the readability and comprehensibility of your code. When someone reads your code, they should be able to understand the purpose and functionality of variables, functions, and classes just by looking at their names. Well-chosen names eliminate ambiguity and reduce the need for comments to explain the code's intent.

Consider the following code snippet:

```python
# Unclear Variable Names

a = 5

b = 10

# Function with Ambiguous Name

def foo(x):

return x * 2
```

In this unclean code, the variable names a and b provide no information about their purpose, and the function name foo is vague. Clean code would use more descriptive names:

 # Improved Variable Names

initial_balance = 5

final_balance = 10

 # Descriptive Function Name

def double_value(value):

return value * 2

With better names, it is clear that initial_balance and final_balance represent financial values, and double_value is a function that doubles its input.

2.1.2 Documentation Through Naming

Well-chosen names act as self-documentation for your code. They convey the "what" and "why" of code elements, reducing the need for extensive comments. Clean code uses names that reveal the purpose, usage, and context of variables and functions. This makes it easier for developers to work with the code, especially when they revisit it after some time.

2.1.3 Maintainability

Maintaining code is a significant part of the software development process. When you use meaningful names, maintenance becomes more efficient. Developers can quickly identify the purpose of variables and functions, making it easier to debug issues, make updates, or add new features.

2.1.4 Reducing Cognitive Load

Clear and meaningful names reduce cognitive load on developers. When names are cryptic or unclear, developers must expend extra mental effort to decipher the code's intent. This cognitive load can lead to errors and slow down the development process. Clean code lightens this cognitive load by using names that convey meaning at a glance.

2.1.5 Consistency and Conventions

Clean code follows consistent naming conventions throughout the codebase. Consistency in naming makes it easier for developers to navigate and understand the code. It's essential to establish naming conventions and adhere to them to maintain uniformity in your projects.

 # Example of Consistent Naming Convention (CamelCase)

customerName = "John Doe"

orderTotalAmount = 100.50

In this example, CamelCase is used consistently for variable names.

In summary, the importance of good names in clean code cannot be overstated. Meaningful names enhance readability, comprehension, and maintainability, reducing cognitive load and promoting consistency. When choosing names, aim for clarity, specificity, and relevance to the code element's purpose. As we delve further into this chapter, we will explore additional guidelines and best practices for choosing effective names in different contexts.

2.2 Choosing Descriptive and Pronounceable Names

In clean code, choosing names that are both descriptive and pronounceable is a fundamental practice. Descriptive names convey the purpose and meaning of code elements, making it easier for developers to understand and work with the code. Pronounceable names facilitate communication among team members and promote a shared understanding of the codebase. In this section, we'll explore the importance of these two aspects in more detail.

2.2.1 Descriptive Names

Descriptive names provide clarity about the purpose and functionality of code elements. When you encounter a variable, function, or class with a descriptive name, you should be able to understand its role without needing additional comments or context. Descriptive names reduce ambiguity and improve code readability.

Consider a variable representing the number of days until a project deadline:

 # Unclear Variable Name

d = 7

In this unclean code, the variable name d provides no information about its purpose. Clean code would use a more descriptive name:

 # Descriptive Variable Name

days_until_deadline = 7

Now, it's evident that days_until_deadline represents the number of days remaining until the project deadline.

2.2.2 Pronounceable Names

Pronounceable names are names that can be easily spoken aloud and understood during discussions or code reviews. When team members can pronounce and discuss code elements fluently, it promotes effective communication. This is especially important in collaborative development environments.

Consider a class name that represents user credentials:

 # Unclear and Unpronounceable Class Name

Crdntl = ...

 # Pronounceable Class Name

UserCredentials = ...

In the first unclean code example, the class name Crdntl is neither descriptive nor pronounceable. In the clean code example, the class is named UserCredentials, which is both descriptive and easy to pronounce.

2.2.3 Meaningful Variable Names

Descriptive and pronounceable names should be applied to variables, constants, and other data elements. Meaningful variable names provide context and convey the purpose of data within the code. Whether it's a loop counter, a configuration setting, or a result variable, meaningful names make code more self-explanatory.

 # Unclear Variable Names

x = 5 *# What does x represent?*

 # Meaningful Variable Names

number_of_attempts = 5 # *Clearly indicates the purpose*

In clean code, variables like number_of_attempts are preferred because they explicitly state their purpose.

2.2.4 Method and Function Names

Method and function names should also be descriptive and pronounceable. They should clearly indicate what the function does or what action it performs. When a developer reads a method or function name, they should immediately grasp its intended behavior.

 # Unclear Function Name

def foo(x):

...

 # Descriptive Function Name

def calculate_total_price(base_price, tax_rate, discount_percentage):

...

In the clean code example, the function calculate_total_price has a descriptive name that conveys its purpose, making it easy to understand its role in the code.

2.2.5 Class and Object Names

Class and object names should follow the same principles. They should be both descriptive and pronounceable. When developers work with classes and objects, the names should provide a clear indication of their responsibilities and roles within the application.

 # Unclear Class Name

class Abc:

...

 # Descriptive Class Name

class OrderProcessor:

...

In clean code, classes like OrderProcessor are preferred because their names communicate their purpose effectively.

In conclusion, choosing descriptive and pronounceable names is a critical aspect of clean code. It enhances code readability, reduces ambiguity, and promotes effective communication within development teams. When naming code elements, aim for clarity, specificity, and ease of pronunciation. By adhering to these principles, you can create code that is not only functional but also understandable and maintainable by both current and future developers.

2.3 Avoiding Disinformation and Misleading Names

In the world of clean code, choosing appropriate names goes beyond just being descriptive and pronounceable; it also involves avoiding names that can mislead or provide incorrect information. Disinformation and misleading names can lead to confusion, errors, and unexpected behavior in your code. In this section, we'll explore the importance of avoiding such names and provide guidance on making choices that reduce the likelihood of misinterpretation.

2.3.1 Misleading Names Can Be Dangerous

Misleading names are names that suggest a different purpose or behavior than what the code element actually represents. When developers encounter such names, they may make incorrect assumptions about the code's functionality, leading to bugs and misunderstandings.

Consider an example where a variable is named tax_rate, but it actually represents the tax amount:

 # Misleading Variable Name

tax_rate = 0.15

total_tax = income * tax_rate

In this unclean code, the variable tax_rate is misleading because it implies that it represents the tax rate as a percentage (e.g., 15%). However, it is actually used as the tax amount (e.g., $15). This can lead to incorrect calculations and misunderstandings.

2.3.2 Be Precise and Specific

To avoid disinformation and misleading names, it's crucial to be precise and specific in your naming choices. Names should accurately represent the purpose and behavior of code elements. If a variable represents a tax amount, it should be named accordingly to avoid any confusion.

 # Precise and Specific Variable Name

tax_amount = 15

total_tax = income * tax_amount

In this clean code example, the variable tax_amount clearly indicates that it represents the tax amount in dollars.

2.3.3 Be Wary of Abbreviations and Acronyms

Abbreviations and acronyms can be a source of confusion, especially when they are not universally understood. Avoid cryptic abbreviations that require developers to guess their meaning. If you must use an abbreviation or acronym, make sure it is well-known in the context of your codebase.

 # Unclear Abbreviation

str = "Hello, World!"

 # Clear Abbreviation

message = "Hello, World!"

In the clean code example, using the variable name message is clearer than the unclear abbreviation str.

2.3.4 Consistency Matters

Consistency in naming conventions across your codebase is essential for avoiding disinformation. When code elements have consistent naming patterns, developers can make informed assumptions about their behavior based on their names.

 # Inconsistent Naming

def getUserData():

...

def retrieve_client_information():

...

In this unclean code, the inconsistent naming of functions (getUserData and retrieve_client_information) can lead to confusion. Clean code would ensure that similar functions have consistent naming patterns.

2.3.5 Use Domain-Specific Language

Whenever possible, use domain-specific language (DSL) in your naming choices. DSL aligns the code with the language used in your project's problem domain, making it more intuitive and reducing the likelihood of disinformation.

 # General Terminology

def process_data(data):

...

 # Domain-Specific Language

def calculate_invoice_total(invoice):

...

In clean code, using domain-specific language like calculate_invoice_total makes the function's purpose clear within the context of an invoicing application.

2.3.6 Seek Feedback

When in doubt about the appropriateness of a name, seek feedback from team members. Code reviews are an excellent opportunity to gather input on naming choices. Developers with different perspectives may provide valuable insights into potential issues with names that could lead to disinformation.

In conclusion, avoiding disinformation and misleading names is a critical aspect of clean code. Names should accurately and clearly represent the purpose and behavior of code elements. Being precise, avoiding cryptic abbreviations, maintaining consistency, and using domain-specific language can help you choose names that reduce the risk of misinterpretation and make your codebase more understandable and reliable. By prioritizing thoughtful naming, you can contribute to the overall quality of your code and enhance collaboration within your development team.

2.4 Using Names that Reveal Intent

One of the fundamental principles of clean code is that names should not only be descriptive but should also reveal the intent behind code elements. When developers read your code, they should not only understand what it does but also why it does it. In this section, we'll explore the importance of using names that convey intent and provide guidelines for achieving this goal.

2.4.1 Code as Documentation

Code should be self-documenting to the extent possible. When you choose names that reveal intent, you turn your code into a form of documentation. Developers can grasp the purpose and motivation behind code elements without the need for extensive comments or additional explanations.

Consider a function that calculates the total price of items in a shopping cart:

 # Unclear Function Name

```
def calculate_total(cart):
```

```
...
```

```
# Function Name Revealing Intent
```

```
def calculate_total_price_of_items(cart):
```

```
...
```

In the clean code example, the function name calculate_total_price_of_items not only describes what the function does but also reveals its intent—to calculate the total price of items in the cart.

2.4.2 Intent-Driven Naming

When choosing names, consider the intent of the code element. What problem does it solve? What role does it play in the broader context of the application? Intent-driven naming focuses on capturing these aspects in the names of variables, functions, classes, and other code elements.

```
# Unclear Variable Name
```

```
result = process_data(data)
```

```
# Intent-Revealing Variable Name
```

```
total_sales = calculate_total_sales(sales_data)
```

In the clean code example, the variable name total_sales is intent-revealing, indicating that it holds the total sales amount.

2.4.3 Choose Verbs and Nouns Thoughtfully

Verbs and nouns are essential elements in intent-revealing names. Verbs in function and method names indicate actions, while nouns in variable and class names represent entities or concepts. By choosing these parts of speech thoughtfully, you can make your code's intent clear.

```python
# Unclear Function Name

def process(data):

...

# Verb and Noun in Function Name

def calculate_total_price(cart):

...

# Unclear Variable Name

t = 0

# Noun in Variable Name

total_price = 0
```

In clean code, using verbs like "calculate" and nouns like "total_price" helps reveal the intent behind code elements.

2.4.4 Avoid Generic Names

Generic names like "temp," "value," or "data" should be avoided as they provide little to no information about the purpose or role of the code element. Instead, choose names that are specific to the context and intent of the code.

 # Unclear Variable Name

temp = calculate_temporary_value()

 # Specific Variable Name

discount_amount = calculate_discount()

In the clean code example, using a specific variable name like discount_amount makes it clear what the variable represents and its intent.

2.4.5 Maintainability and Understanding

Using names that reveal intent enhances the maintainability of your code. When you revisit code after some time or when another developer works with it, the intent-revealing names make it easier to understand the code's purpose and behavior. This, in turn, reduces the likelihood of introducing errors during maintenance.

2.4.6 Refactoring with Confidence

Intent-revealing names also facilitate refactoring. When you decide to refactor or modify code, having clear and intention-revealing names provides a safety net. You can make changes confidently, knowing that the code's intent remains intact and that it's less likely to break.

In conclusion, using names that reveal intent is a core practice of clean code. These names transform your code into self-documentation, making it understandable to both you and your fellow developers. By considering the intent behind code elements and choosing verbs and nouns thoughtfully, you can create code that is not only functional but also expressive and maintainable. Intent-driven naming is a powerful tool for improving code quality and ensuring that your codebase remains comprehensible and robust over time.

2.5 Making Meaningful Distinctions in Names

In the pursuit of clean code, it's crucial to make meaningful distinctions in names, especially when dealing with multiple code elements that serve similar purposes. Meaningful distinctions help developers differentiate between variables, functions, classes, or other code elements, reducing confusion and potential errors. In this section, we'll delve into the significance of making meaningful distinctions in names and provide guidance on how to achieve this effectively.

2.5.1 Avoid Ambiguity

Ambiguity in names can lead to confusion and errors. When two or more code elements have similar names that don't provide meaningful distinctions, developers may inadvertently use the wrong element, leading to unexpected behavior or bugs.

Consider two variables representing different types of taxes:

 # Ambiguous Variable Names

tax = 0.15

sales_tax = 0.08

In this unclean code, the names tax and sales_tax are ambiguous, as they both appear to represent taxes. To avoid ambiguity, make meaningful distinctions in names:

 # Meaningfully Distinguished Variable Names

income_tax_rate = 0.15

sales_tax_rate = 0.08

Now, it's clear that income_tax_rate and sales_tax_rate represent different types of taxes.

2.5.2 Use Context for Distinctions

Context is a powerful tool for making meaningful distinctions in names. Consider the context in which a code element is used and choose a name that reflects its role and purpose within that context.

 # Unclear Variable Names Without Context

price = 100

total = price * quantity

 # Meaningfully Distinguished Variable Names with Context

item_price = 100

total_price = item_price * quantity

In the clean code example, the variables item_price and total_price are named within the context of an item's price and the total price, making their distinctions clear.

2.5.3 Add Qualifiers

Adding qualifiers to names is an effective way to make meaningful distinctions. Qualifiers can be prefixes, suffixes, or additional words that provide context and specificity to a code element.

 # Unclear Variable Names Without Qualifiers

size = 10

```
max_size = 20
```

```
# Meaningfully Distinguished Variable Names with Qualifiers
```

```
initial_size = 10
```

```
maximum_size = 20
```

In the clean code example, the qualifiers "initial" and "maximum" clarify the distinctions between the variables.

2.5.4 Avoid Overloading Names

Overloading names occurs when a single name is used for multiple code elements with different purposes or contexts. This can lead to confusion and unexpected behavior.

```
# Overloaded Function Name
```

```
def calculate_total(price):
```

```
...
```

```
def calculate_total(items):
```

```
...
```

In this unclean code, the function name calculate_total is overloaded with two different meanings. To make meaningful distinctions, use unique names for different code elements:

```
# Meaningfully Distinguished Function Names
```

```
def calculate_total_price(price):
```

```
...
```

```
def calculate_total_items(items):
```

...

Now, it's clear that calculate_total_price and calculate_total_items serve different purposes.

2.5.5 Maintain a Consistent Approach

Consistency in making distinctions is essential. When you establish a naming convention or pattern for making distinctions in names, stick to it throughout your codebase. Consistency reduces cognitive load and helps developers quickly understand the code.

 # Inconsistent Naming Conventions

order_number = 123

customerID = "ABC123"

 # Consistent Naming Conventions

order_number = 123

customer_id = "ABC123"

In clean code, using consistent naming conventions, such as using underscores for multi-word names, enhances readability and maintainability.

2.5.6 Prioritize Clarity

While making meaningful distinctions is essential, prioritizing clarity is equally important. Names should not be overly long or convoluted, as they can become difficult to work with. Balance meaningful distinctions with brevity and readability.

In summary, making meaningful distinctions in names is a vital aspect of clean code. It reduces ambiguity, prevents errors, and enhances code readability. By avoiding ambiguity, using context, adding qualifiers, and maintaining consistency, you can create code that is not only functional but also easy to understand and maintain. Prioritizing clarity in your naming choices ensures that your code remains comprehensible and efficient, benefiting both current and future developers working on the codebase.

Chapter 3: Functions

3.1 The Role of Functions in Clean Code

Functions are fundamental building blocks in software development, and their role in clean code is of paramount importance. Clean functions are small, focused, and do one thing well. They contribute to code readability, maintainability, and testability. In this section, we'll explore the significance of functions in clean code and delve into the principles that guide their design and implementation.

3.1.1 Functions as Abstractions

Functions serve as abstractions that encapsulate specific actions or behaviors within your code. They allow you to break down complex tasks into manageable, reusable units. Well-designed functions act as black boxes, providing a clear interface for other parts of the code to interact with.

```python
# Unclean Code with Complex Logic

def calculate_total_price(items, tax_rate, discount_percentage):

# Complex logic for calculating total price

...
```

In this unclean code example, the calculate_total_price function is burdened with complex logic. Clean code prefers to abstract this logic into smaller, focused functions:

```python
# Clean Code with Abstractions

def calculate_total_price(items, tax_rate, discount_percentage):
```

```
subtotal = calculate_subtotal(items)

total_with_tax = apply_tax(subtotal, tax_rate)

total_with_discount       =       apply_discount(total_with_tax, discount_percentage)

return total_with_discount
```

Clean code breaks down the calculation into smaller functions like calculate_subtotal, apply_tax, and apply_discount, making the code more readable and maintainable.

3.1.2 Small and Focused Functions

Clean code adheres to the principle that functions should be small and focused, with a single responsibility. This practice, often referred to as the Single Responsibility Principle (SRP), ensures that functions are easy to understand and modify.

 # Unclean Function with Multiple Responsibilities

```
def process_order(order):

validate_order(order)

calculate_total_price(order)

save_order_to_database(order)
```

In this unclean code, the process_order function has multiple responsibilities, making it less maintainable and more error-prone. Clean code divides these responsibilities into separate functions:

 # Clean Code with Small and Focused Functions

```
def process_order(order):
```

validate_order(order)

total_price = calculate_total_price(order)

save_order_to_database(order, total_price)

By splitting the responsibilities into distinct functions, clean code adheres to the SRP, enhancing readability and maintainability.

3.1.3 Function Names and Readability

Function names play a critical role in clean code. A well-chosen name should convey the function's purpose and behavior. Clean code favors descriptive and intention-revealing function names.

 # Unclear Function Name

def xyz(a, b, c):

...

 # Descriptive Function Name

def calculate_average_score(scores):

...

In the clean code example, the function calculate_average_score has a descriptive name that immediately communicates its purpose.

3.1.4 Function Arguments and Side Effects

Clean functions minimize the number of arguments they accept and aim to have as few side effects as possible. Functions with numerous arguments or functions that modify external states can become challenging to reason about and test.

 # Function with Many Arguments

```python
def process_data(data, settings, logger, database_connection):
```

...

 # Function with Side Effects

```python
def save_data(data):
```

...

In clean code, functions are designed to be more self-contained, reducing their dependencies and side effects:

 # Clean Code with Minimal Arguments and Side Effects

```python
def process_data(data):
```

...

```python
def save_data_to_database(data):
```

...

By keeping function arguments to a minimum and minimizing side effects, clean code enhances predictability and testability.

3.1.5 Encapsulation and Reusability

Clean code leverages functions for encapsulation and reusability. Functions encapsulate behavior, making it easier to change or extend functionality without affecting the entire codebase. Reusable functions promote DRY (Don't Repeat Yourself) principles, reducing code duplication.

 # Unclean Code with Redundant Logic

```python
if condition:
```

```python
perform_action_1()
else:
perform_action_2()

# Clean Code with Encapsulation and Reusability

def perform_action():
...
if condition:
perform_action_1()
else:
perform_action_2()
```

In the clean code example, a single perform_action function encapsulates the behavior, eliminating redundancy and promoting reusability.

In summary, functions are essential components of clean code that promote abstraction, encapsulation, and reusability. Clean functions are small, focused, and follow the SRP. They have descriptive names, minimize arguments, and reduce side effects. By adhering to these principles, clean code enhances code readability, maintainability, and testability, contributing to the overall quality of the software.

3.2 Small and Focused Functions

Small and focused functions are a cornerstone of clean code. They adhere to the Single Responsibility Principle (SRP), which states that a function should have one clear and well-defined responsibility. In this section, we'll dive deeper into the importance of small and focused functions, their benefits, and how to achieve them effectively.

3.2.1 The Single Responsibility Principle (SRP)

The SRP, one of the SOLID principles of object-oriented programming, emphasizes that a function should have only one reason to change. This means that a function should encapsulate a single piece of behavior or functionality. When a function has multiple responsibilities, it becomes harder to understand, modify, and maintain.

Consider an unclean function that performs both data validation and data processing:

 # Unclean Function with Multiple Responsibilities

def process_data(data):

if is_valid(data):

perform_processing(data)

In this unclean code, the process_data function has two responsibilities: data validation and data processing. This violates the SRP and makes the function less clean.

3.2.2 Benefits of Small and Focused Functions

Small and focused functions offer several benefits:

1. Improved Readability:

Small functions are easier to read and understand. When a function has a clear and singular purpose, developers can quickly grasp its intent without getting bogged down in unrelated details.

2. Enhanced Maintainability:

Functions with a single responsibility are easier to modify and maintain. When you need to make changes, you can focus on a specific area of code without worrying about unintended consequences.

3. Reusability:

Small functions are more reusable. When a function performs a well-defined task, it can be easily reused in different parts of your codebase, reducing redundancy and promoting DRY (Don't Repeat Yourself) principles.

4. Testability:

Small functions are easier to test. Testing becomes more straightforward when you can isolate a specific behavior or functionality within a function and write targeted test cases for it.

5. Collaboration:

Clean code with small and focused functions encourages collaboration within development teams. Developers can work on individual functions independently without stepping on each other's toes.

3.2.3 Guidelines for Creating Small and Focused Functions

To create small and focused functions, consider the following guidelines:

1. Choose Descriptive Names:

Give your functions descriptive names that clearly convey their purpose. A well-chosen name should make it evident what the function does without the need for extensive comments.

 # Unclear Function Name

```python
def process(data):
```

...

 # Descriptive Function Name

```python
def validate_data(data):
```

...

In the clean code example, the function validate_data has a descriptive name that reveals its purpose.

2. Follow the SRP:

Ensure that each function has a single responsibility. If a function performs multiple tasks, consider refactoring it into smaller functions, each with a distinct purpose.

 # Function with Multiple Responsibilities

```python
def process_order(order):

validate_order(order)

calculate_total_price(order)

save_order_to_database(order)
```

In clean code, the responsibilities are divided into separate functions like validate_order, calculate_total_price, and save_order_to_database.

3. Limit Function Length:

Keep functions concise and focused. While there is no strict rule for the number of lines a function should have, a common guideline is to aim for functions that can be read and understood in one screen without scrolling.

 # Long Function

def process_data(data):

...

...

...

 # Small and Focused Function

def validate_data(data):

...

In clean code, small and focused functions like validate_data are easier to understand and maintain.

4. Minimize Side Effects:

Reduce side effects within functions. Side effects, such as modifying global variables or external states, can make functions less predictable and harder to reason about.

 # Function with Side Effects

def update_database(data):

...

global_variable = result

...

 # Function with Minimal Side Effects

def process_data(data):

...

result = perform_processing(data)

return result

Clean code minimizes side effects and encapsulates behavior within functions, enhancing predictability.

In summary, small and focused functions are a fundamental aspect of clean code. They adhere to the Single Responsibility Principle and offer benefits such as improved readability, maintainability, reusability, testability, and collaboration. By following guidelines that prioritize descriptive names, the SRP, function length, and side effect minimization, you can create functions that are not only clean but also efficient and easy to work with.

3.3 Function Arguments and Side Effects

In clean code, careful consideration is given to function arguments and side effects. Function arguments are the parameters that a function accepts, and side effects are the changes a function makes to the program's state outside of its scope. Clean functions aim to minimize both the number of arguments they accept and their side effects. In this section, we'll explore the significance of these aspects and how they contribute to clean code.

3.3.1 Minimizing Function Arguments

Clean code strives to minimize the number of function arguments for several reasons:

1. Readability:

Functions with fewer arguments are more readable. When a function has many arguments, it can become challenging to understand its purpose and behavior.

 # Function with Many Arguments

```python
def calculate_total_price(item, tax_rate, discount_percentage, shipping_fee):
    ...
```

In this unclean code, the function calculate_total_price has four arguments, making it less readable.

2. Maintainability:

Functions with fewer arguments are easier to maintain. When you need to make changes to a function, you have fewer variables to consider, reducing the risk of introducing errors.

3. Testability:

Functions with fewer arguments are more testable. Writing test cases for functions with numerous arguments can become cumbersome. With fewer arguments, you can write more focused and manageable tests.

4. Flexibility:

Functions with fewer arguments are more flexible and adaptable. They are less tied to specific data structures or dependencies, making them easier to reuse in different contexts.

Clean code achieves these benefits by encapsulating related data into objects or using default values and optional arguments when appropriate:

```python
# Clean Code with Encapsulation

class Order:

    def __init__(self, item, tax_rate, discount_percentage, shipping_fee):

        self.item = item

        self.tax_rate = tax_rate

        self.discount_percentage = discount_percentage

        self.shipping_fee = shipping_fee

    def calculate_total_price(order):

        ...
```

In this clean code example, related data is encapsulated into an Order object, reducing the number of function arguments in calculate_total_price.

3.3.2 Minimizing Side Effects

Clean functions aim to minimize side effects, which are changes made to the program's state outside of the function's scope. Excessive side effects can lead to unpredictable behavior and make code harder to reason about. Functions that modify global variables, manipulate external states, or have hidden consequences can be problematic.

 # Function with Side Effects

def update_global_variable(data):

global_variable = data

...

 # Function with Hidden Side Effect

def process_data(data):

...

result = perform_processing(data)

...

In this unclean code, the functions update_global_variable and process_data have side effects that may not be immediately apparent. Clean code minimizes side effects by clearly specifying the function's behavior and avoiding unexpected changes to the program's state.

3.3.3 Emphasizing Pure Functions

Pure functions are functions that have no side effects and produce the same output for the same input every time they are called. Clean code encourages the use of pure functions whenever possible. Pure functions are predictable, testable, and can be safely parallelized, making them a valuable component of clean code.

 # Pure Function

```python
def calculate_total_price(item_price, tax_rate, discount_percentage):

subtotal = item_price * (1 - discount_percentage)

total_price = subtotal * (1 + tax_rate)

return total_price
```

In this clean code example, the calculate_total_price function is a pure function because it takes inputs, performs calculations, and returns an output without modifying external states.

3.3.4 Function Signatures and Documentation

Clean code places emphasis on clear function signatures and documentation. A function's signature, including its name and parameter names, should provide a clear indication of its purpose and behavior. Additionally, documenting a function's intended behavior, its input parameters, and return values helps developers understand how to use it correctly.

 # Clean Function with Clear Signature and Documentation

```python
def calculate_total_price(item_price: float, tax_rate: float, discount_percentage: float) -> float:
```

```
"""
```

Calculates the total price of an item after applying tax and discount.

Args:

item_price (float): The price of the item before tax and discount.

tax_rate (float): The tax rate as a decimal (e.g., 0.08 for 8% tax).

discount_percentage (float): The discount percentage as a decimal (e.g., 0.10 for 10% discount).

Returns:

float: The total price of the item after tax and discount.

```
"""
```

```python
subtotal = item_price * (1 - discount_percentage)

total_price = subtotal * (1 + tax_rate)

return total_price
```

In this clean code example, the function signature and documentation provide a clear understanding of the function's purpose, arguments, and return value.

3.3.5 Achieving Clean and Predictable Code

In summary, clean code emphasizes the minimization of function arguments and side effects. By encapsulating related data, using pure functions, and providing clear function signatures and documentation, you can create code that is clean, predictable, and easier to read, maintain, and test. Clean code reduces the risk of unexpected behavior and enhances the overall quality and reliability of your software.

3.4 Command Query Separation

Clean code adheres to the principle of Command Query Separation (CQS), which states that a function should either be a command or a query but not both. Commands are functions that perform an action and do not return a value, while queries are functions that return a value and do not modify the program's state. Separating commands from queries enhances code clarity, predictability, and maintainability.

3.4.1 Commands

Commands, also known as mutators, are functions that perform actions or modify the program's state but do not return a value. They are responsible for changing the internal state of objects, writing to databases, sending emails, or performing any action that does not involve retrieving data.

```python
# Command (Mutator) Function

def add_to_cart(item, cart):

cart.add(item)
```

In this example, the add_to_cart function is a command because it adds an item to the cart but does not return any information.

3.4.2 Queries

Queries are functions that return information or data but do not modify the program's state. They are responsible for retrieving data from objects, databases, or external sources without causing any side effects.

 # Query Function

def calculate_total_price(items):

total = 0

for item **in** items:

total += item.price

return total

The calculate_total_price function is a query because it computes and returns the total price of items without modifying any state.

3.4.3 Benefits of CQS

Command Query Separation offers several benefits:

1. Clarity:

CQS enhances code clarity by clearly distinguishing between functions that change state and functions that retrieve data. This separation makes code easier to understand and reason about.

2. Predictability:

CQS promotes predictability in code behavior. When you see a function, you can quickly determine whether it performs an action or returns a value, reducing surprises and unexpected side effects.

3. Testability:

Separating commands from queries simplifies testing. Queries are naturally testable because they return values that can be asserted, while commands can be tested for their actions and side effects.

4. Debugging:

Debugging is more straightforward when commands and queries are separated. You can isolate the source of issues and identify whether they result from actions or data retrieval.

3.4.4 CQS in Practice

To apply CQS effectively, follow these guidelines:

1. Clearly Indicate Intent:

Use function names and documentation to clearly indicate whether a function is a command or a query. Descriptive names and documentation help developers understand a function's purpose and behavior.

2. Avoid Hybrid Functions:

Avoid creating functions that mix commands and queries. A function should either change state (command) or retrieve data (query) but not both.

3. Minimize Side Effects:

Commands should minimize side effects and clearly communicate any changes they make to the program's state. Avoid hidden or unexpected side effects.

4. Favor Immutability:

When designing objects or data structures, favor immutability for query methods. Immutability ensures that queries do not inadvertently modify objects.

5. Isolate Commands and Queries:

In code organization, group commands and queries separately. This makes it easier to locate and reason about functions with similar roles.

```python
# Grouping Commands and Queries

class ShoppingCart:

def __init__(self):

self.items = []

def add_item(self, item):

...

def remove_item(self, item):

...

def calculate_total_price(self):
```

...

In this clean code example, commands (e.g., add_item and remove_item) and queries (e.g., calculate_total_price) are grouped within the ShoppingCart class.

Command Query Separation is a fundamental principle of clean code that enhances code clarity, predictability, testability, and maintainability. By clearly distinguishing between commands and queries and following best practices, you can create code that is easier to understand, debug, and maintain, ultimately improving the quality and reliability of your software.

3.5 Error Handling in Functions

Clean code places significant importance on error handling within functions. Error handling is the process of managing and responding to unexpected or erroneous conditions that can occur during the execution of a function. Proper error handling contributes to code reliability, robustness, and maintainability. In this section, we'll explore the principles and best practices of error handling in functions.

3.5.1 The Nature of Errors

Errors can take various forms, including runtime exceptions, invalid input, network failures, and resource unavailability. They can originate from external sources, user interactions, or internal logic. Recognizing the different types of errors is crucial for effective error handling.

```python
# Handling Invalid Input

def divide(a, b):
```

if b == 0:

raise ValueError("Division by zero is not allowed.")

return a / b

In this example, the divide function handles the error of division by zero by raising a ValueError.

3.5.2 Error Handling Strategies

Clean code employs error handling strategies that prioritize clarity and maintainability. Common strategies include:

1. Propagation:

In some cases, functions may not handle errors themselves but propagate them to their callers. This allows higher-level code to handle errors appropriately.

def process_data(data):

if not is_valid(data):

raise ValueError("Invalid data.")

 # Continue processing

The process_data function propagates the error to its caller by raising a ValueError when data is invalid.

2. Graceful Degradation:

In situations where errors are expected or recoverable, clean code employs graceful degradation. Instead of throwing exceptions, functions gracefully handle errors and provide fallback behavior or informative messages.

```python
def read_file(filename):

try:

with open(filename, "r") as file:

return file.read()

except FileNotFoundError:

return "File not found."
```

The read_file function gracefully handles the FileNotFoundError by returning an informative message instead of raising an exception.

3. Logging and Reporting:

Clean code emphasizes the use of logging and reporting mechanisms to capture error information. Logging helps developers diagnose issues, and reporting ensures that stakeholders are informed about errors.

```python
import logging

def perform_operation(data):

try:

# Perform operation

except Exception as e:

logging.error(f"An error occurred: {str(e)}")

raise
```

The perform_operation function logs error information using the Python logging module before re-raising the exception.

3.5.3 Using Exceptions for Error Handling

Clean code favors the use of exceptions for error handling. Exceptions provide a structured way to handle errors, propagate them, and differentiate between different error types.

```python
def calculate_division(a, b):

try:

result = a / b

except ZeroDivisionError:

raise ValueError("Division by zero is not allowed.")

return result
```

In this example, the calculate_division function uses a try...except block to handle the ZeroDivisionError and raise a ValueError with a more informative message.

3.5.4 Wrapping External Dependencies

When working with external dependencies, clean code often wraps them to provide better control over error handling and to decouple the code from specific implementations. Wrapping external dependencies also enables unit testing with mock objects.

```python
import requests

def fetch_data(url):

try:
```

```python
response = requests.get(url)

response.raise_for_status() # Raise an exception for non-2xx status codes

return response.json()

except (requests.exceptions.RequestException, ValueError) as e:

logging.error(f"An error occurred while fetching data: {str(e)}")

return None
```

In this example, the fetch_data function wraps the requests library and provides error handling for network-related issues and JSON parsing errors.

3.5.5 Avoiding Null References

Clean code aims to minimize the use of null references or null values as error indicators. Instead, it prefers to use exceptions or other error-handling mechanisms to signify and handle errors explicitly.

```python
# Unclean Code with Null Reference

def find_user(username):

user = database.query(username)

if user is None:

return "User not found."

return user

# Clean Code with Exception Handling

def find_user(username):
```

```python
try:

user = database.query(username)

return user

except DatabaseError:

raise ValueError("An error occurred while querying the database.")
```

In the clean code example, the find_user function raises a ValueError in case of a database error, making the error explicit.

In summary, clean code prioritizes proper error handling within functions. It recognizes the nature of errors, employs error handling strategies such as propagation, graceful degradation, and logging, and uses exceptions to handle errors in a structured manner. Wrapping external dependencies and avoiding null references help create robust and maintainable code that is resilient to unexpected conditions and errors. Proper error handling contributes to code reliability and enhances the overall quality of the software.

Chapter 4: Comments

4.1 When to Write Comments

Comments play a role in code documentation and communication, providing explanations, clarifications, and context to readers, including other developers who work on the codebase. However, clean code emphasizes that comments should be used judiciously and for specific purposes. In this section, we'll explore when to write comments and the principles that guide their effective use.

4.1.1 Providing Clarification

Comments are valuable when they clarify code that might be confusing or unclear without additional context. If a piece of code performs a non-obvious or intricate operation, a comment can help explain the logic and the underlying reasoning.

 # Calculate the average score

average_score = sum(scores) / len(scores)

In this example, the comment provides clarity by explaining the purpose of the code, making it easier for readers to understand that it calculates the average score.

4.1.2 Documenting Intent

Comments are essential for documenting the intent behind a piece of code. They answer the question of "why" something is being done. This is especially valuable for complex algorithms, optimizations, or workarounds.

 # Use a binary search for performance optimization

```
result = binary_search(sorted_array, target)
```

In this case, the comment explains that a binary search is chosen for performance optimization, which helps readers understand the rationale behind the choice.

4.1.3 Explaining Non-Obvious Decisions

Comments can justify non-obvious decisions or deviations from typical coding practices. When code follows a unique or unconventional approach, comments help others understand the reasoning behind it.

```
# Using a custom hashing function for better collision handling

hashed_key = custom_hash(key)
```

This comment justifies the use of a custom hashing function, which might not be the default choice, by emphasizing its advantages in collision handling.

4.1.4 Describing Complex Algorithms

Complex algorithms or data structures often require detailed explanations. Comments can provide step-by-step descriptions of the algorithm's logic or data structure's operations, making it easier for others to follow the code.

```
# Dijkstra's algorithm for finding the shortest path in a graph

def dijkstra(graph, start_node):

    ...
```

The comment clarifies that the function implements Dijkstra's algorithm, which is a non-trivial algorithm for finding the shortest path in a graph.

4.1.5 Warning about Known Issues

When code contains known issues, limitations, or temporary workarounds, comments are crucial for warning others about these issues. This helps prevent misconceptions and encourages transparency.

 # Workaround: This library has a memory leak issue with version 2.1. Avoid using until it's resolved.

import problematic_library

In this case, the comment warns developers about a known memory leak issue in a specific library version.

4.1.6 Keeping Comments Up-to-Date

It's important to note that comments can become outdated if code evolves over time. Clean code encourages developers to keep comments synchronized with the code. When code changes, developers should review and update comments accordingly to ensure accuracy.

In summary, clean code suggests that comments should be used to provide clarification, document intent, explain non-obvious decisions, describe complex algorithms, warn about known issues, and offer explanations where code alone may not suffice. Comments should be concise, focused, and aligned with the code's evolution. Overreliance on comments to compensate for poorly written code should be avoided, as clean code aims to make the code itself as self-explanatory as possible.

4.2 Good Comments vs. Bad Comments

Comments are a valuable tool in code, but not all comments are created equal. Clean code distinguishes between good comments that enhance understanding and bad comments that can clutter code and create confusion. In this section, we'll explore the characteristics of good and bad comments and the principles to guide their use effectively.

4.2.1 Good Comments

Good comments serve specific purposes that contribute positively to code readability and maintenance:

1. Explanation and Clarification:

Good comments explain code that may be unclear or confusing to others. They provide context and help readers understand the code's logic or purpose.

 # Initialize the counter to zero

counter = 0

In this example, the comment provides a straightforward explanation of why the counter is being initialized to zero.

2. Documentation of Complex Logic:

Good comments document complex algorithms, calculations, or data structures. They break down intricate operations into manageable steps, making the code more understandable.

 # Perform matrix multiplication using the Strassen algorithm

result = strassen_matrix_multiply(matrix1, matrix2)

The comment here documents the use of the Strassen algorithm for matrix multiplication, which might be non-trivial to grasp from the code alone.

3. Legal or Licensing Information:

Comments that contain legal or licensing information are good comments. They ensure compliance with open-source licenses or copyright requirements.

 # Licensed under the MIT License. See LICENSE.txt for details.

Including a licensing comment helps clarify the terms under which the code can be used.

4. TODO and Future Improvements:

Good comments also include "TODO" or "FIXME" markers to highlight areas where improvements or additional work is needed in the future. These comments serve as reminders for developers.

*# **TODO**: Refactor this code for better performance*

The "TODO" comment indicates that there's room for improvement in the code.

4.2.2 Bad Comments

While comments can be beneficial, bad comments can clutter code and hinder comprehension. Clean code identifies several types of bad comments to avoid:

1. Redundant Comments:

Redundant comments restate the obvious and do not add any value to the code. They can make the code unnecessarily verbose.

 # This is a for loop

```
for i in range(10):
    ...
```

This comment is redundant and does not provide any useful information beyond what the code itself conveys.

2. Outdated Comments:

Outdated comments are comments that are no longer accurate or relevant due to code changes. Keeping outdated comments can lead to confusion.

 # To-do: Fix the bug in the next release

If the bug mentioned in the comment has already been fixed, it becomes outdated and misleading.

3. Excessive Comments:

Excessive comments occur when there is an over-reliance on comments to explain every line of code, even when the code is self-explanatory.

 # Increment the counter

```
counter += 1
```

In this case, the comment merely repeats what the code does, adding unnecessary clutter.

4. Commented-Out Code:

Commented-out code should be avoided in most cases. It clutters the codebase and can make it difficult to distinguish between active and inactive code.

 # This code is no longer used

 # counter -= 1

Instead of commenting out code, it's better to use version control systems to track changes and preserve previous code versions.

5. Cryptic Comments:

Cryptic or unclear comments, which are difficult to understand or contain abbreviations or acronyms without explanation, should be avoided.

 # Calculate the ROR

ror = (revenue - cost) / cost

The abbreviation "ROR" may not be clear to all readers, making the comment cryptic.

4.2.3 Principles for Effective Comments

To use comments effectively in clean code, consider the following principles:

1. Be Concise and Specific:

Write comments that are concise and directly related to the code they explain. Avoid excessive verbosity or unrelated information.

2. Keep Comments Updated:

Regularly review and update comments to ensure they remain accurate and relevant, especially when code changes occur.

3. Prioritize Self-Explanatory Code:

Strive to write code that is self-explanatory through meaningful variable and function names, and only use comments when necessary to provide additional context.

4. Use Comments as a Last Resort:

Use comments as a last resort when it's not possible to make the code itself clearer through improvements in naming, structure, or organization.

5. Avoid Commented-Out Code:

Remove or refactor commented-out code, as it can create confusion and clutter. Use version control systems for historical code tracking.

In summary, clean code recognizes that comments can be a valuable asset when used effectively to clarify code, document complex logic, indicate licensing information, or highlight areas for future improvement. However, it also emphasizes the importance of avoiding bad comments that are redundant, outdated, excessive, or cryptic. Clean code strives for code that is self-explanatory, minimizing the need for comments while ensuring that the comments that are used serve a clear and meaningful purpose.

4.3 Writing Self-Explanatory Code

Clean code promotes the idea that code should be as self-explanatory as possible without relying heavily on comments. Self-explanatory code is code that is clear, readable, and easy to understand without the need for extensive comments. In this section, we'll explore the principles and techniques for writing self-explanatory code.

4.3.1 Meaningful Variable and Function Names

One of the fundamental principles of self-explanatory code is using meaningful variable and function names. Well-chosen names can convey the purpose and intent of the code, making comments less necessary.

```
# Unclear Variable Names

a = 10

b = 5

result = a + b

# Self-Explanatory Variable Names

total_score = 10

bonus_points = 5

final_score = total_score + bonus_points
```

In the second example, meaningful variable names like total_score and bonus_points make it clear what the code is doing.

4.3.2 Consistent Naming Conventions

Clean code adheres to consistent naming conventions throughout the codebase. This consistency helps developers quickly grasp the meaning of variables and functions.

 # Inconsistent Naming

user_name = "John"

userAge = 30

 # Consistent Naming (CamelCase)

user_name = "John"

user_age = 30

Consistent use of naming conventions, such as CamelCase for variables and functions, enhances code readability.

4.3.3 Avoiding Magic Numbers and Strings

Magic numbers and strings are hard-coded values scattered throughout the code without explanation. Clean code recommends replacing magic numbers and strings with named constants or variables to make the code self-explanatory.

 # Magic Number

if temperature > 32:

...

 # Self-Explanatory Code with Constants

FREEZING_POINT = 32

if temperature > FREEZING_POINT:

...

Incorporating named constants like FREEZING_POINT provides clarity and context to the code.

4.3.4 Clear and Logical Code Structure

A well-structured codebase follows logical patterns and organization. Clean code breaks down complex functionality into smaller, focused functions and classes, each with a clear responsibility.

 # Unclear Code Structure

def process_data(data):

...

 # Complex logic

...

 # Self-Explanatory Code Structure

class DataProcessor:

def __init__(self, data):

self.data = data

def process(self):

...

 # Clear and focused logic

...

The second example exhibits a self-explanatory code structure with a class designed for data processing.

4.3.5 Avoiding Nested and Complex Conditionals

Clean code discourages the use of deeply nested and complex conditional statements. Instead, it suggests breaking down complex logic into smaller, well-named functions and using clear boolean expressions.

 # Nested Conditionals

if condition1:

if condition2:

if condition3:

...

 # Self-Explanatory Code with Functions

if is_condition_met():

...

The use of functions like is_condition_met() simplifies code by abstracting complex logic.

4.3.6 Documentation as a Supplement

While self-explanatory code is the primary goal, clean code acknowledges that there are situations where documentation is necessary. In such cases, comments should serve as supplements to explain why specific design decisions were made or to document complex algorithms. However, the code itself should remain the primary source of understanding.

 # Comment as a Supplement

def calculate_discount(price):

 # Apply a 10% discount for loyalty members

...

In this example, the comment supplements the code by explaining the reason behind the discount.

4.3.7 Code Reviews and Collaboration

Code reviews are an essential part of maintaining self-explanatory code. Collaborative efforts among developers can lead to improvements in code clarity, naming, and structure. Encouraging team members to provide feedback and suggestions during code reviews helps ensure code remains self-explanatory.

In summary, clean code places a strong emphasis on writing self-explanatory code that is clear, readable, and easy to understand without excessive reliance on comments. This is achieved through meaningful variable and function names, consistent naming conventions, the elimination of magic numbers and strings, clear code structure, and avoidance of nested and complex conditionals. While documentation in the form of comments can be useful, it should be a supplement rather than a crutch. Clean code fosters collaboration and code reviews as means to continually improve code clarity and maintain self-explanatory code.

4.4 Using Comments to Clarify Intent

While clean code strives for code that is self-explanatory, there are situations where comments are valuable for providing additional context and clarifying the intent behind certain code segments. In this section, we'll explore how comments can be effectively used to explain why specific design decisions were made or to provide insights into complex algorithms.

4.4.1 Explaining Design Decisions

Comments can be instrumental in explaining the rationale behind design decisions, especially when there are multiple valid approaches to solving a problem. By clarifying why a particular design was chosen, comments help other developers understand the thought process.

```
# Using a list comprehension for performance optimization

squared_numbers = [x ** 2 for x in numbers]
```

In this comment, the developer explains that a list comprehension was chosen for performance optimization, providing insight into the decision-making process.

4.4.2 Documenting Algorithm Insights

Complex algorithms may benefit from comments that document key insights or steps in the algorithm. This documentation helps others follow the logic and understand the algorithm's inner workings.

```
# Step 1: Initialize the data structures

# Step 2: Perform a depth-first search to find connected components

# Step 3: Compute properties of the connected components
```

These comments outline the high-level steps of an algorithm, making it easier for developers to grasp its operation.

4.4.3 Warning About Side Effects

Comments can serve as warnings about potential side effects or consequences of code execution. When code has unexpected or non-obvious outcomes, comments can alert other developers to these effects.

 # Caution: This function modifies the global variable 'data_cache'

def process_data(data):

...

The comment provides a cautionary note about the function's impact on the global variable 'data_cache.'

4.4.4 Temporary Workarounds

In some cases, code may include temporary workarounds or solutions to known issues. Comments can explain these workarounds and indicate that they are not the final solution.

 # Workaround for a bug in LibraryX version 2.1. Remove this when upgrading to 2.2.

import LibraryX

This comment documents the temporary nature of the workaround and the intention to remove it in a future library upgrade.

4.4.5 Historical Context

Code often evolves over time, and comments can provide historical context about why certain decisions were made. This context helps developers understand the evolution of the codebase.

 # Originally implemented for compatibility with legacy systems

def legacy_function():

...

The comment explains that the function was initially implemented for compatibility with legacy systems, shedding light on its historical significance.

4.4.6 Best Practices for Comment Clarity

To effectively use comments to clarify intent, consider the following best practices:

1. Be Concise and Focused:

Comments should be concise and focused on the specific aspect they are explaining. Avoid verbosity or unrelated information.

2. Use Clear Language:

Use clear and plain language in comments, avoiding jargon or technical terms that may not be universally understood.

3. Update Comments with Code Changes:

As code evolves, make sure to update comments to reflect changes in design decisions or algorithm implementations.

4. Avoid Redundant Comments:

Comments that merely repeat what the code does should be avoided. Comments should provide insights that are not immediately apparent from the code itself.

5. Use a Consistent Comment Style:

Adopt a consistent comment style, such as starting comments with a capital letter and ending with a period, to maintain readability and consistency.

In summary, clean code recognizes that while self-explanatory code is the primary goal, comments can be instrumental in providing context and clarifying the intent behind specific code segments. Comments are used to explain design decisions, document algorithm insights, warn about side effects, indicate temporary workarounds, and offer historical context. Effective comments are concise, clear, and focused, serving as valuable supplements to the codebase's understanding and maintenance.

4.5 Avoiding Redundant Comments

Clean code advocates for the use of comments to enhance code understanding and provide valuable context when necessary. However, it also emphasizes the importance of avoiding redundant comments that do not contribute to comprehension and may even clutter the codebase. In this section, we'll explore the concept of redundant comments and why they should be minimized.

4.5.1 Redundant Comments Defined

Redundant comments are comments that duplicate information already evident from the code itself. They don't provide any additional insights or explanations beyond what the code clearly conveys. Redundant comments can be detrimental to code readability and maintainability.

 # Increment the counter

counter += 1

In this example, the comment merely repeats what the code does, making it redundant.

4.5.2 The Problem with Redundant Comments

Redundant comments can introduce several problems:

1. Code Clutter:

Excessive comments that reiterate what the code does can clutter the codebase, making it harder to read and understand.

2. Maintenance Overhead:

Redundant comments require maintenance effort to keep them synchronized with code changes. When code evolves, developers must remember to update the comments, adding unnecessary overhead.

3. Risk of Contradiction:

Redundant comments can inadvertently contradict the code when they become outdated or inconsistent with the code's behavior. This can lead to confusion.

4. Reduced Trust in Comments:

When developers encounter many redundant comments, they may become conditioned to ignore comments altogether, potentially missing valuable insights in genuinely informative comments.

4.5.3 When Are Comments Redundant?

Identifying redundant comments can be subjective and context-dependent. However, some common scenarios where comments are often redundant include:

1. Self-Explanatory Code:

When the code itself is clear and self-explanatory through meaningful names and logical structure, additional comments that merely restate the code's functionality can be redundant.

 # Calculate the sum of 'a' and 'b'

result = a + b

In this case, the comment doesn't provide any valuable information beyond what the code demonstrates.

2. Obvious Logic:

Comments that describe straightforward or universally understood logic are often redundant. Code should strive to be clear without the need for such comments.

 # Check if 'x' is greater than 10

if x > 10:

...

The comment here doesn't add value as the condition's intent is evident.

3. Repetitive Comments:

When similar comments are repeated throughout the codebase, conveying the same information, they are redundant. It's more efficient to consolidate such information in a single location.

4.5.4 Guidelines for Reducing Redundant Comments

To reduce redundant comments and maintain clean code, consider the following guidelines:

1. Prioritize Self-Explanatory Code:

Strive to write code that is self-explanatory through meaningful names, clear logic, and a well-structured design. Minimize the need for comments by making the code itself as understandable as possible.

2. Eliminate Obvious Comments:

Review the codebase for comments that describe evident logic or actions. Remove or replace these comments with more valuable explanations or insights.

3. Consolidate Information:

When multiple similar comments exist, consolidate the information into a single, central location. This reduces redundancy and ensures that updates are made consistently.

4. Encourage Peer Reviews:

Incorporate code reviews into the development process. Encourage team members to identify and address redundant comments during reviews.

5. Use Comments Sparingly:

While comments play a vital role in code documentation, use them sparingly and purposefully. Reserve comments for situations where they genuinely enhance code understanding or provide valuable context.

In summary, clean code promotes the avoidance of redundant comments that do not contribute to code comprehension and may hinder it. Redundant comments can clutter the codebase, introduce maintenance overhead, risk contradictions, and reduce trust in comments. Developers are encouraged to prioritize self-explanatory code, eliminate obvious comments, consolidate information when possible, and use comments sparingly and purposefully. The goal is to maintain code that is both readable and maintainable, without unnecessary commentary.

Chapter 5: Formatting

5.1 Code Formatting and Readability

Clean code places a significant emphasis on code formatting and readability. Code is written and structured in a way that makes it easy for developers to understand, maintain, and collaborate on. In this section, we'll delve into the importance of code formatting and explore best practices for enhancing code readability.

5.1.1 The Significance of Code Formatting

Code formatting encompasses various aspects, including indentation, spacing, line length, and the use of consistent conventions. It plays a crucial role in code readability and maintenance for several reasons:

1. Improved Understanding:

Well-formatted code is easier to understand at a glance. Proper indentation and consistent spacing help developers identify code blocks, loops, and conditionals quickly.

2. Reduced Bugs:

Clear formatting reduces the likelihood of introducing syntax errors or logic bugs due to misaligned code. It promotes better code quality.

3. Enhanced Collaboration:

When code follows consistent formatting standards, it's more accessible for multiple developers to collaborate on a project. A unified coding style makes it easier for team members to work together seamlessly.

4. Easier Maintenance:

Maintaining properly formatted code is less error-prone and requires less effort. Developers can make changes or fix issues more confidently and efficiently.

5.1.2 Consistency Matters

Consistency in code formatting is a fundamental principle of clean code. Clean code adheres to a set of agreed-upon formatting conventions and standards throughout the codebase. These conventions may include:

- **Indentation**: Whether to use tabs or spaces and the number of spaces for each level of indentation.

- **Spacing**: Guidelines for spacing around operators, commas, and brackets.

- **Line Length**: Limits on the maximum line length to ensure code fits within a readable width.

- **Naming Conventions**: Rules for naming variables, functions, classes, and other code elements.

 # Inconsistent Indentation

```
def example_function():

if condition:

statement1
```

```
else:

statement2

# Consistent Indentation

def example_function():

if condition:

statement1

else:

statement2
```

In this example, consistent indentation improves code readability.

5.1.3 Code Formatting Tools

Clean code often employs automated code formatting tools and linters to enforce consistent formatting across the codebase. These tools can automatically correct formatting issues, ensuring that the code adheres to the defined conventions.

Popular code formatting tools for various programming languages include:

- **Python**: Black, autopep8, and YAPF

- **JavaScript/TypeScript**: Prettier, ESLint, and TSLint

- **Java**: Checkstyle and Google Java Format

- **C++**: Clang-Format and Uncrustify

Using these tools as part of the development workflow helps maintain clean and consistently formatted code.

5.1.4 Comments and Formatting

Clean code also acknowledges the relationship between comments and code formatting. Comments should be properly aligned and formatted to enhance readability. They should be concise, clear, and follow consistent formatting standards.

Correctly Formatted Comment

This is a comment explaining the purpose of the code.

Poorly Formatted Comment

This is a comment explaining the purpose of the code.

Consistently formatted comments contribute to overall code clarity and professionalism.

5.1.5 Practical Tips for Code Formatting

To ensure clean and readable code, consider the following practical tips:

1. Follow a Style Guide:

Adopt a coding style guide or use the conventions established by the programming community for your chosen language.

2. Use an Editor or IDE Extension:

Leverage code editors or integrated development environments (IDEs) that support code formatting extensions or plugins. These tools can automatically format code as you write or save it.

3. Configure Linters:

Set up linters to catch formatting issues and enforce coding standards. Linters can provide immediate feedback and flag inconsistencies.

4. Collaborate on Formatting Standards:

Work with your development team to define and agree upon code formatting standards. Consensus on conventions promotes consistency.

5. Review and Refactor:

Regularly review your code for formatting discrepancies and refactor as needed. Clean up any inconsistencies to maintain readability.

In conclusion, clean code recognizes that code formatting and readability are essential for software development. Proper formatting improves code understanding, reduces errors, enhances collaboration, and simplifies maintenance. Consistency in formatting conventions is vital, and the use of automated tools and linters can help enforce these standards. By following best practices and collaborating with your team, you can ensure that your code remains clean, readable, and maintainable.

5.2 The Importance of Consistency

Consistency is a fundamental aspect of clean code. In the context of code formatting, consistency means adhering to a set of rules and conventions throughout the codebase. Clean code places a strong emphasis on consistency because it contributes significantly to code readability and maintainability.

5.2.1 Consistency in Indentation

One of the most noticeable aspects of code formatting is indentation. Indentation is used to visually represent the structure of the code, including loops, conditionals, and function definitions. Consistent indentation makes it easy for developers to understand the code's hierarchy.

Inconsistent indentation can lead to confusion, making it challenging to discern the relationships between code blocks. Clean code promotes the adoption of a specific indentation style and ensuring that it's applied consistently.

```
# Inconsistent Indentation

def example_function():

if condition:

statement1

else:

statement2

# Consistent Indentation

def example_function():

if condition:

statement1

else:

statement2
```

The consistent indentation in the second example enhances code readability and clarity.

5.2.2 Consistency in Spacing

Spacing conventions are another critical aspect of code formatting. Clean code specifies guidelines for spacing around operators, commas, brackets, and other elements. Consistent spacing ensures that code is visually uniform and predictable.

Inconsistent spacing can make code appear cluttered or disorganized. It can also lead to syntax errors or code that behaves unexpectedly.

 # Inconsistent Spacing

result = a +b

 # Consistent Spacing

result = a + b

The consistent spacing in the second example improves code quality and readability.

5.2.3 Consistency in Naming Conventions

Clean code also advocates for consistency in naming conventions. Naming conventions dictate how variables, functions, classes, and other code elements are named. Consistent naming conventions make it easier for developers to understand the purpose and usage of code elements.

Inconsistent naming conventions can result in confusion and difficulty in identifying the roles of different code elements.

 # Inconsistent Naming

user_name = "John"

userAge = 30

 # Consistent Naming (CamelCase)

userName = "John"

userAge = 30

Consistent naming conventions, such as CamelCase for variables and functions, enhance code clarity.

5.2.4 Consistency Across the Codebase

Maintaining consistency across the entire codebase is essential. This consistency should extend beyond individual code files and encompass the entire project. When multiple developers work on a project, adhering to the same formatting standards is crucial for seamless collaboration.

Consistency in code formatting is achieved through the following practices:

1. Style Guides:

Adopting a coding style guide specific to the programming language or framework being used provides a clear set of formatting rules. These style guides are often community-driven and widely accepted.

2. *Automated Formatting Tools:*

Use automated code formatting tools that enforce coding standards. These tools can automatically format code according to the defined conventions.

3. *Linters:*

Integrate linters into the development workflow to catch formatting issues and enforce coding standards. Linters provide immediate feedback and help maintain consistency.

4. *Code Reviews:*

Incorporate code reviews into the development process. Code reviews involve peers checking for adherence to formatting standards and providing feedback.

5. *Team Collaboration:*

Collaborate with the development team to establish and maintain coding conventions. Open communication and consensus on standards are essential.

5.2.5 Benefits of Consistency

Consistency in code formatting offers several benefits:

1. *Improved Readability:*

Consistent formatting makes code more readable and approachable, leading to better understanding.

2. Reduced Errors:

Consistent formatting reduces the likelihood of introducing syntax errors or logic bugs due to formatting discrepancies.

3. Easier Maintenance:

Maintaining consistent code is more straightforward, as developers can follow established patterns without confusion.

4. Effective Collaboration:

Consistency enables effective collaboration among developers, regardless of their individual coding styles.

5. Professionalism:

Consistently formatted code reflects professionalism and attention to detail, which is essential in software development.

In summary, clean code places a high value on consistency in code formatting. Consistency encompasses aspects such as indentation, spacing, naming conventions, and overall style. Adhering to established conventions and using automated tools and linters to enforce coding standards helps maintain consistency. Consistent code formatting enhances readability, reduces errors, simplifies maintenance, facilitates collaboration, and reflects professionalism in software development practices.

5.3 Horizontal Formatting

Horizontal formatting refers to how code is structured and laid out horizontally within a line or statement. Clean code emphasizes the importance of horizontal formatting for code readability and maintainability. In this section, we'll explore best practices and principles related to horizontal code formatting.

5.3.1 Line Length

One key aspect of horizontal formatting is managing line length. Clean code suggests keeping lines of code within a reasonable length to ensure readability. Long lines can be challenging to read, especially when code is viewed on narrower screens or in printed documentation.

A common guideline is to limit lines to a maximum of 80 to 120 characters. However, the specific line length may vary depending on the coding conventions of a particular programming language or project.

 # Long Line (Exceeding Recommended Length)

result = calculate_long_expression(arg1, arg2, arg3, arg4, arg5, arg6, arg7, arg8)

 # Proper Line Length

result = calculate_long_expression(

arg1, arg2, arg3, arg4, arg5, arg6, arg7, arg8

)

In the second example, breaking the long line into multiple lines makes the code more readable and adheres to the recommended line length.

5.3.2 Alignment

Alignment is another horizontal formatting consideration. Clean code suggests aligning related code elements vertically to improve code readability. When multiple lines contain similar elements, aligning them makes it easier to spot patterns and relationships.

Unaligned Code

var1 = 10

var2 = 20

var3 = 30

Aligned Code

var1 = 10

var2 = 20

var3 = 30

In the aligned code example, variables are vertically aligned, enhancing code readability.

5.3.3 Operators and Indentation

Clean code advises that operators should be spaced consistently to improve code readability. Operators include arithmetic operators (+, -, *, /), assignment operators (=), and comparison operators (==, !=, <, >, etc.).

Inconsistent Operator Spacing

result = a+b*2-c

Consistent Operator Spacing

result = a + b * 2 - c

In the second example, consistent operator spacing improves code clarity.

Indentation is another aspect of horizontal formatting that contributes to code readability. Indentation helps visually distinguish code blocks, such as loops and conditionals. Clean code recommends using consistent and meaningful indentation.

 # Inconsistent Indentation

if condition:

statement1

else:

statement2

 # Consistent Indentation

if condition:

statement1

else:

statement2

The second example follows consistent indentation, making the code structure clear.

5.3.4 Long Function Calls

When calling functions with many arguments, clean code suggests formatting the call by placing each argument on a separate line. This makes the code more readable and helps avoid excessively long lines.

 # Long Function Call (Exceeding Recommended Line Length)

result = some_function(arg1, arg2, arg3, arg4, arg5, arg6)

 # Proper Function Call Formatting

result = some_function(

arg1, arg2, arg3, arg4, arg5, arg6

)

In the properly formatted function call, each argument is placed on a separate line, adhering to line length recommendations.

5.3.5 Practical Tips for Horizontal Formatting

To ensure clean and readable horizontal formatting, consider the following practical tips:

1. Use Line Continuation:

For long lines that exceed the recommended length, use line continuation techniques provided by the programming language. This may include using backslashes () or parentheses () to split lines.

 # Line Continuation Using Backslash

result = some_function(arg1, arg2, arg3, \

arg4, arg5)

 # Line Continuation Using Parentheses

result = some_function(

arg1, arg2, arg3,

arg4, arg5

)

2. Choose Meaningful Alignment:

When aligning code elements vertically, choose meaningful alignment points. For example, align variable assignments by their equal signs or align function arguments by their commas.

3. Use Consistent Indentation:

Adopt consistent indentation practices throughout the codebase. Consistency enhances code readability and clarity.

4. Avoid Excessive Nesting:

Excessive levels of indentation and nesting can make code harder to read. Consider refactoring code to reduce nesting when possible.

5. Leverage Code Editors:

Many code editors and integrated development environments (IDEs) offer features that automatically handle indentation and line formatting. Utilize these tools to simplify the process.

In summary, clean code recognizes the importance of horizontal formatting for code readability and maintainability. It advises managing line length, aligning related code elements, spacing operators consistently, using meaningful indentation, and properly formatting long function calls. Adhering to these principles and following practical tips helps developers write code that is clean, organized, and easy to understand.

5.4 Vertical Formatting

Vertical formatting refers to how code is structured and organized vertically within a file or code block. Clean code places a strong emphasis on vertical formatting because it significantly affects code readability, maintainability, and comprehension. In this section, we will explore best practices and principles related to vertical code formatting.

5.4.1 Logical Grouping

Clean code encourages logically grouping related code together. This means that functions, methods, and code blocks should be organized in a way that makes sense in terms of functionality. For example, in object-oriented programming, methods that perform similar tasks or belong to the same class should be grouped together.

```python
# Logical Grouping of Methods

class MyObject:

def __init__(self):

self.data = []

def add_item(self, item):

...

def remove_item(self, item):

...

def process_data(self):

...
```

In this example, methods related to managing MyObject instances are logically grouped within the class definition.

5.4.2 Readable Sections

Clean code promotes the use of clear and descriptive section headers or comments to separate different parts of a file or code block. This helps readers quickly identify the purpose and content of each section. Meaningful section headers can act as a table of contents for the code.

```
# Constants

MAX_RETRY_COUNT = 3

# Data Processing Functions

def process_data(data):

...

# Error Handling

def handle_error(error):

...
```

Descriptive section headers make it easy to locate specific parts of the code and understand their context.

5.4.3 Vertical Density

Clean code advises against overly dense code blocks that cram too much logic into a small vertical space. Code blocks should have enough vertical whitespace to allow for readability. Adequate spacing improves code comprehension and makes it easier to follow the flow of control.

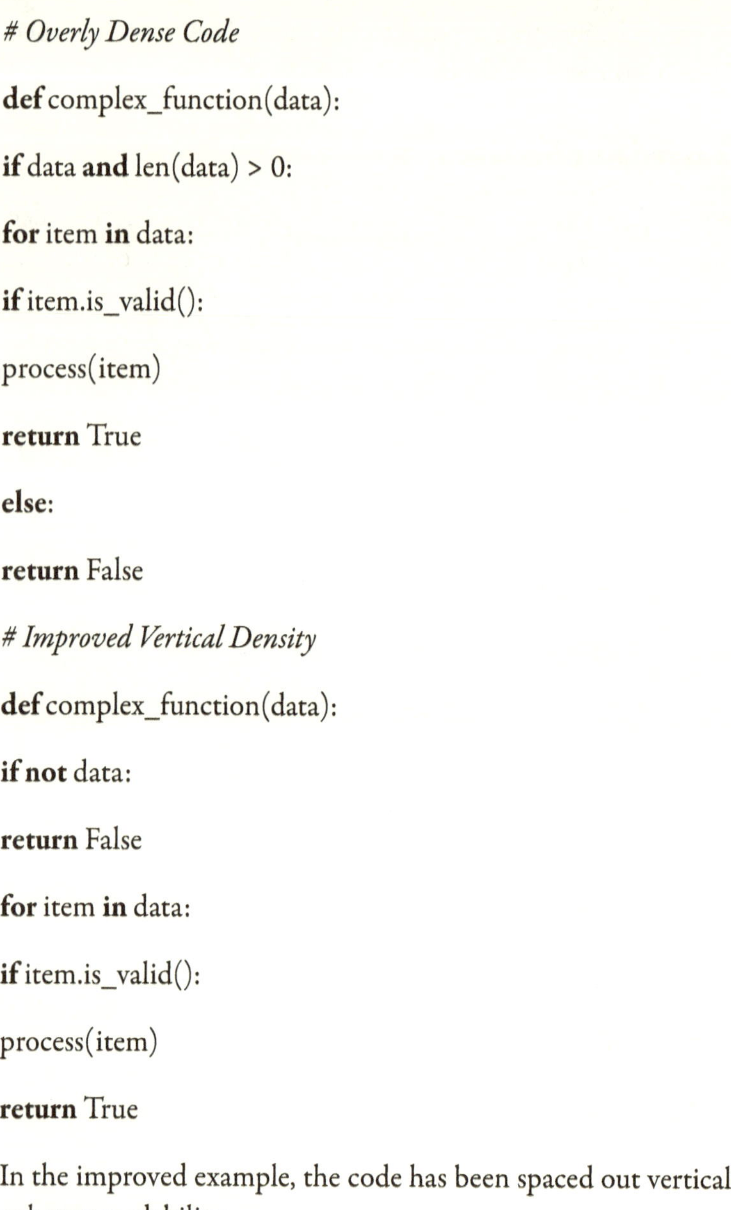

```python
# Overly Dense Code

def complex_function(data):

if data and len(data) > 0:

for item in data:

if item.is_valid():

process(item)

return True

else:

return False

# Improved Vertical Density

def complex_function(data):

if not data:

return False

for item in data:

if item.is_valid():

process(item)

return True
```

In the improved example, the code has been spaced out vertically to enhance readability.

5.4.4 Limited Function and Method Length

Clean code encourages keeping functions and methods concise and focused on a single responsibility. Functions that are too long and perform multiple tasks can be challenging to read and understand. It's recommended to limit the length of functions and methods to improve vertical readability.

```python
# Long Function

def process_data(data):

result = []

for item in data:

if item.is_valid():

temp = item.process()

if temp:

result.append(temp)

return result

# Shorter and Focused Function

def process_data(data):

valid_items = [item.process() for item in data if item.is_valid()]

return [item for item in valid_items if item]
```

In the second example, the function has been refactored into shorter, focused sections for improved vertical readability.

5.4.5 Practical Tips for Vertical Formatting

To ensure clean and readable vertical formatting, consider the following practical tips:

1. Use Descriptive Naming:

Choose clear and descriptive names for functions, methods, variables, and sections. Meaningful names improve code understanding.

2. Follow Consistent Patterns:

Adopt consistent patterns for structuring code vertically. Use a consistent style for section headers, comments, and whitespace.

3. Favor Simplicity:

Strive for simplicity in code organization. Avoid unnecessary complexity and nesting.

4. Refactor as Needed:

Regularly review code and refactor when necessary. Split long functions or methods into smaller, more focused ones.

5. Utilize Vertical Whitespace:

Use vertical whitespace to separate logical blocks of code. Adequate spacing enhances readability.

In summary, clean code places a strong emphasis on vertical formatting to improve code readability and comprehension. It encourages logical grouping of code, the use of readable sections, avoidance of overly dense code, and limiting the length of functions and methods. By following best practices and practical tips for vertical formatting, developers can create clean, organized, and maintainable code.

5.5 Comments and Formatting

Clean code recognizes the crucial relationship between comments and code formatting. While clean code encourages self-explanatory code that minimizes the need for comments, it acknowledges that well-placed and well-formatted comments can enhance code clarity. In this section, we will explore the role of comments in clean code and how they should be integrated into the codebase while considering code formatting.

5.5.1 When to Write Comments

Clean code suggests that comments should be used sparingly and only when necessary. Comments should not be a substitute for writing clean and self-explanatory code. Instead, comments should serve specific purposes:

1. Explanation of Intent:

Comments can be used to explain the intent behind a particular piece of code, especially when the purpose may not be immediately obvious to other developers. This helps readers understand why a certain approach was taken.

 # Initialize the counter variable

counter = 0

In this example, the comment clarifies the purpose of initializing the counter variable.

2. Documentation of Complex Algorithms:

When implementing complex algorithms or data structures, comments can provide a high-level overview of the algorithm's logic. This can help developers understand the algorithm's strategy without delving into the intricate details.

 # Quick Sort Algorithm Implementation

 # 1. Choose a pivot element.

 # 2. Partition the array around the pivot.

 # 3. Recursively sort the sub-arrays.

In this case, the comments offer a concise summary of the Quick Sort algorithm.

3. Explanation of Non-Obvious Decisions:

When making non-obvious decisions or workarounds due to specific constraints or edge cases, comments can clarify the reasoning behind these choices.

 # Workaround for issue #12345: Forced conversion to string to prevent type error.

result = str(some_variable)

Here, the comment explains why a forced conversion to a string is being used.

4. API Documentation:

When defining functions, classes, or methods that are part of an API, clean code recommends using comments to provide clear and concise documentation of their usage, parameters, and return values. This helps other developers who will use the API understand how to use it correctly.

5.5.2 Good Comments vs. Bad Comments

Clean code distinguishes between good comments that enhance code understanding and bad comments that add noise or duplicate information. To ensure that comments are valuable, consider the following guidelines:

Good Comments:

- **Concise and Clear**: Good comments are concise and to the point, providing valuable information without unnecessary verbosity.

- **Maintained**: Comments should be kept up-to-date. If code changes, comments should be revised accordingly to reflect the current state.

- **Relevant**: Comments should focus on important aspects of the code, such as its purpose, assumptions, or potential side effects.

Bad Comments:

- **Redundant**: Comments that simply restate what the code already expresses clearly can be redundant and add clutter.

- **Obsolete**: Comments that are no longer relevant due to code changes should be removed or updated.

- **Inconsistent**: Inconsistent or misleading comments can cause confusion and should be avoided.

5.5.3 Writing Self-Explanatory Code

Clean code promotes the idea that the best way to improve code readability is to write self-explanatory code. Self-explanatory code makes comments unnecessary because the code itself clearly conveys its purpose.

To achieve self-explanatory code:

- Use meaningful variable, function, and class names.

- Break down complex logic into smaller, well-named functions or methods.

- Eliminate redundancy and duplication.

- Follow consistent coding conventions.

```
# Non-Self-Explanatory Code

if x % 2 == 0:  # Check if x is even

print("Even")
```

```
else:

print("Odd")
```

 # Self-Explanatory Code

```
if is_even(x):

print("Even")

else:

print("Odd")
```

In the self-explanatory code example, the function is_even makes the code's intent clear, reducing the need for a comment.

5.5.4 Avoiding Redundant Comments

Clean code advises against using comments that reiterate what the code already expresses. Redundant comments can lead to inconsistencies and confusion if the code is modified but the comments are not updated.

 # Calculate the sum of a and b

```
result = a + b
```

In this case, the comment is redundant because the code itself makes it evident that the sum of a and b is being calculated.

5.5.5 Comment Formatting

When writing comments, clean code suggests following consistent formatting standards. Consistency in comment formatting contributes to code professionalism and readability.

 # Good Comment Formatting

 # This is a well-formatted comment that explains the code's purpose.

 # Bad Comment Formatting

 # This comment has inconsistent spacing and is harder to read.

In the good comment formatting example, proper spacing and clear formatting enhance readability.

5.5.6 Commenting for Future Developers

Clean code acknowledges that code may be read and maintained by developers who did not originally write it. Therefore, comments should be written with future developers in mind. Comments should help them quickly grasp the code's functionality, intent, and any potential pitfalls.

5.5.7 Documentation Tools

In addition to inline comments, clean code recommends using documentation tools and formats that generate external documentation from code comments. Popular documentation tools, such as Sphinx for Python or Javadoc for Java, allow developers to create structured and searchable documentation directly from code comments.

5.5.8 Practical Tips for Commenting

To effectively use comments in clean code:

- Prioritize writing self-explanatory code to minimize the need for comments.

Chapter 6: Objects and Data Structures

6.1 Objects vs. Data Structures

In the realm of software design, two fundamental concepts play crucial roles: objects and data structures. These two concepts represent different philosophies when it comes to organizing and modeling data within a program. In this section, we'll explore the distinctions between objects and data structures, their strengths, and their appropriate use cases.

6.1.1 Objects

Objects are a cornerstone of object-oriented programming (OOP). They encapsulate both data and the operations that can be performed on that data. An object combines attributes (data fields) and methods (functions) into a cohesive unit, allowing data and the behavior that operates on it to be closely tied together.

In OOP, objects are instances of classes. Classes define the structure and behavior of objects, acting as blueprints for creating instances. Objects hide their internal implementation details and expose a well-defined interface for interacting with them.

 # Example of an Object

```python
class Circle:

def __init__(self, radius):

self.radius = radius

def area(self):

return 3.141592653589793 * self.radius ** 2
```

```python
# Creating an instance of the Circle class

my_circle = Circle(5)

# Using the object's methods

circle_area = my_circle.area()
```

In this example, Circle is a class that defines a circle object. The object my_circle has both data (the radius attribute) and behavior (the area method) associated with it.

6.1.2 Data Structures

Data structures, on the other hand, are a fundamental concept in non-object-oriented programming paradigms, such as procedural or functional programming. Data structures are containers for storing and organizing data, but they lack the behavior that objects possess. Data structures expose the data they contain but do not include methods that operate on that data.

```python
# Example of a Data Structure (Dictionary)

student = {

"name": "Alice",

"age": 25,

"grade": "A",

}

# Accessing data in the dictionary

student_name = student["name"]
```

In this example, student is a dictionary data structure containing key-value pairs. It stores data but does not have methods associated with it.

6.1.3 Strengths of Objects

Objects offer several strengths:

1. **Encapsulation**: Objects encapsulate data and behavior together, hiding internal details and exposing a well-defined interface. This encapsulation promotes information hiding and reduces complexity.
2. **Abstraction**: Objects abstract away implementation details, allowing users to interact with them at a higher level of abstraction. This simplifies the usage of complex systems.
3. **Polymorphism**: Objects can exhibit polymorphic behavior, where different objects of the same class can respond differently to the same method call. Polymorphism enables flexible and extensible designs.

6.1.4 Strengths of Data Structures

Data structures also have their strengths:

1. **Simplicity**: Data structures are often simpler to understand and use, especially for storing and retrieving data. They are suitable for scenarios where behavior is minimal, and the focus is on data organization.
2. **Performance**: Data structures can be highly optimized for specific data access patterns. They are efficient for operations like searching, sorting, and iteration.
3. **Interoperability**: Data structures are often more interoperable with other programming languages or

systems. They can be easily serialized and deserialized for data exchange.

6.1.5 Choosing Between Objects and Data Structures

The choice between objects and data structures depends on the goals and requirements of your software design:

- Use objects when you want to encapsulate both data and behavior, promote abstraction, and achieve polymorphic behavior. Objects are suitable for modeling complex real-world entities and implementing business logic.

- Use data structures when your primary focus is on organizing and accessing data efficiently. Data structures are appropriate for cases where behavior is minimal, and you need simplicity and performance.

In practice, a well-designed software system often combines both objects and data structures to leverage their respective strengths. This hybrid approach allows you to represent data in the most suitable form for different parts of your application while maintaining clean and modular code.

Remember that the choice between objects and data structures is a design decision, and there is no one-size-fits-all answer. It should align with the overall architecture and objectives of your software project.

6.2 The Law of Demeter

The Law of Demeter, often referred to as the "Principle of Least Knowledge," is a design guideline in object-oriented programming that promotes loose coupling and encapsulation. It states that an object should only interact with its immediate neighbors and should not have knowledge of the internal workings of other objects beyond its immediate scope.

6.2.1 Understanding the Law of Demeter

The Law of Demeter can be summarized by the following principles:

1. **Talk to friends, not strangers**: An object should only call methods of its own:

 # Violation of the Law of Demeter

class Order:

def calculate_total(self, customer, shipping_address):

 # ...

price = customer.get_product_price(product)

 # ...

In this example, the Order class directly interacts with the customer object, violating the Law of Demeter. Instead, it should communicate with its immediate collaborators or request only the information it needs.

1. **Don't reach too deep**: Avoid chaining method calls on objects:

 # Violation of the Law of Demeter

user_profile   =
user.get_profile().get_address().get_zip_code()

In this example, the code makes a series of method calls on different objects. This tightly couples the calling code to the internal structure of these objects.

1. **Use parameters**: Pass necessary information as parameters rather than navigating through objects:

 # Applying the Law of Demeter

class Order:

def calculate_total(self, product_price):

...

price = product_price

...

In this modified code, the calculate_total method receives the product_price as a parameter instead of obtaining it indirectly from other objects. This reduces the coupling between the Order class and other classes.

6.2.2 Benefits of the Law of Demeter

Adhering to the Law of Demeter offers several advantages:

• **Reduced Coupling**: By limiting an object's interactions to its immediate collaborators, you reduce the dependencies between objects. This leads to a more modular and maintainable codebase.

• **Improved Encapsulation**: Objects maintain their encapsulation because they do not expose their internal structure to other objects. This encapsulation enhances information hiding and simplifies changes to an object's implementation.

• **Enhanced Testability**: Code that adheres to the Law of Demeter is often easier to test since you can substitute mock or stub objects for dependencies without affecting the calling code.

• **Flexibility**: Loose coupling and reduced knowledge of internal details make the code more flexible and adaptable to changes. Modifying the internals of an object does not ripple through the entire system.

6.2.3 Applying the Law of Demeter

To apply the Law of Demeter effectively, consider the following strategies:

1. **Limit method chaining**: Avoid chaining method calls on multiple objects. Instead, break down complex operations into smaller, self-contained steps.
2. **Use parameters**: Pass necessary data and dependencies as parameters to methods rather than retrieving them from other objects.
3. **Delegate responsibilities**: Encapsulate interactions with other objects within dedicated methods. This way, the object can manage its collaborations without exposing them.
4. **Favor interfaces**: Interact with objects through interfaces or abstractions rather than concrete implementations. This reduces the dependency on specific classes.
5. **Review and refactor**: Regularly review your codebase to

identify violations of the Law of Demeter and refactor them to adhere to the principle.

In summary, the Law of Demeter encourages a design that promotes loose coupling, encapsulation, and maintainability in object-oriented systems. By following these principles, you can create more modular and flexible code that is easier to understand and maintain.

6.3 Data Transfer Objects (DTOs)

Data Transfer Objects (DTOs) are a design pattern used in software engineering to efficiently transfer data between different parts of an application or between different applications. DTOs are lightweight, plain data containers that carry data between layers or components of a system. They serve as a convenient way to package and transport data without exposing the internal details of the objects they represent.

6.3.1 Purpose of Data Transfer Objects

The primary purpose of DTOs is to solve the problem of data transmission between different parts of an application, especially in scenarios where:

1. **Data Format Transformation**: The data format or structure expected by one part of the system is different from the format in which the data is available in another part. DTOs help transform data from one format to another.
2. **Reducing Network Calls**: In distributed systems or microservices architectures, reducing the number of network calls is essential for performance optimization.

DTOs allow bundling multiple data items into a single request or response, reducing the number of network requests.

3. **Security and Privacy**: DTOs can be used to exclude sensitive or unnecessary data when transmitting information over a network. This ensures that only relevant data is shared.

4. **Versioning**: When an application evolves and the structure of data changes, DTOs can provide a versioning mechanism. Old clients can continue using older DTO versions while new clients adopt the latest versions.

6.3.2 Characteristics of Data Transfer Objects

DTOs typically exhibit the following characteristics:

• **No Behavior**: DTOs are passive data structures with no behavior. They contain fields (attributes) to store data but do not have methods or logic associated with them.

• **Serializable**: DTOs are often designed to be serializable, meaning they can be converted to a format suitable for transmission over a network, such as JSON or XML.

• **Immutable**: DTOs are usually designed as immutable objects. Once created, their state cannot be changed. This ensures that the data remains consistent during transmission.

6.3.3 Example of Data Transfer Objects

Let's consider a simple example of a DTO used for transferring user data from a client to a server in a web application:

```python
# Data Transfer Object (DTO) for User Information

class UserDTO:

def __init__(self, username, email, age):

self.username = username

self.email = email

self.age = age

# Usage of the UserDTO

user_data = UserDTO("john_doe", "john@example.com", 30)
```

In this example, UserDTO is a plain Python class with fields for username, email, and age. It serves as a container for transferring user-related data between client and server components. The data is encapsulated within the DTO, and it can be serialized and sent over the network.

6.3.4 Drawbacks and Considerations

While DTOs are useful for data transmission, they also have some drawbacks and considerations:

- **Boilerplate Code**: Creating DTOs often requires writing repetitive code to define the fields and constructors, which can be seen as boilerplate.

- **Maintaining Synchronization**: As the application evolves, DTOs may need to be kept in sync with changes in the data model. This maintenance overhead can be a challenge.

- **Data Transformation Overhead**: Transforming data between DTOs and the application's domain objects can introduce computational overhead, especially in complex systems.

- **Increased Complexity**: Overusing DTOs can lead to a proliferation of data structures, potentially increasing the complexity of the codebase.

Despite these considerations, when used judiciously, DTOs are a valuable tool for addressing data transfer and integration challenges in software systems. They help maintain separation of concerns, improve data integrity, and enhance the performance and scalability of distributed applications.

6.4 Active Objects

Active Objects is a design pattern that combines the benefits of both objects and data structures to create a flexible and efficient way to manage concurrent operations and asynchronous tasks. This pattern is particularly useful when dealing with scenarios where multiple threads or processes need to perform operations concurrently while preserving data integrity.

6.4.1 Key Concepts of Active Objects

Active Objects introduce the following key concepts:

1. **Object-like Encapsulation**: Active Objects encapsulate both data and behavior, similar to traditional objects. This encapsulation allows them to maintain internal state and execute operations on that state.
2. **Concurrency Control**: Active Objects employ mechanisms to ensure safe concurrent access to their

internal state. This can include using locks, mutexes, or other synchronization techniques to prevent data corruption.

3. **Asynchronous Execution**: Active Objects typically allow clients to submit tasks or requests for execution asynchronously. These tasks are then scheduled and processed by the active object's internal threads or mechanisms.

6.4.2 Use Cases for Active Objects

Active Objects are particularly suitable for scenarios where:

- **Concurrency**: Multiple threads or processes need to access and modify shared data concurrently, and data integrity must be maintained.

- **Asynchronous Operations**: Operations or tasks can be performed asynchronously to improve responsiveness and resource utilization.

- **Resource Management**: Active Objects can help manage limited resources, such as connections to databases or external services, efficiently.

- **Event Handling**: Systems that handle events, notifications, or messages from external sources can benefit from the event-driven nature of active objects.

6.4.3 Implementing Active Objects

Implementing an active object involves several steps:

1. **Encapsulation**: Define a class that encapsulates both the

data and behavior that need to be protected. This class will be the active object.

2. **Concurrency Control**: Implement mechanisms for concurrency control to ensure that multiple threads or processes can safely access and modify the internal state. This may involve using locks, semaphores, or other synchronization primitives.

3. **Asynchronous Execution**: Create a mechanism for clients to submit tasks or requests to the active object for asynchronous execution. These tasks are typically added to a queue and processed by the active object's internal threads.

4. **Execution Loop**: Implement an execution loop within the active object that continuously processes tasks from the queue. This loop should handle exceptions and errors gracefully.

Here's a simplified Python example of an active object:

```python
import threading

from queue import Queue

class ActiveObject:

    def __init__(self):

        self.internal_state = 0

        self.task_queue = Queue()

        self.lock = threading.Lock()

        self.worker_thread = threading.Thread(target=self._process_tasks)

        self.worker_thread.start()
```

```python
def _process_tasks(self):

while True:

task = self.task_queue.get()

if task is None:

break

with self.lock:

# Perform the task while protecting internal state

self.internal_state += task

self.task_queue.task_done()

def perform_operation(self, value):

# Submit a task for asynchronous execution

self.task_queue.put(value)

def stop(self):

# Signal the worker thread to exit

self.task_queue.put(None)

self.worker_thread.join()
```

In this example, the ActiveObject class encapsulates an internal_state and allows clients to submit tasks using perform_operation. The worker_thread continuously processes tasks from the queue, ensuring that the internal_state is modified safely.

6.4.4 Benefits and Considerations

Active Objects offer several benefits:

- **Concurrent Data Access**: They enable concurrent access to data while maintaining data integrity through synchronization mechanisms.

- **Asynchronous Execution**: Active Objects can execute tasks asynchronously, improving system responsiveness and resource utilization.

- **Resource Management**: They can efficiently manage resources, such as connections or threads.

However, implementing active objects can be complex and may introduce overhead due to synchronization. Careful design and consideration of concurrency issues are necessary to ensure the correctness and efficiency of active object implementations.

Active Objects are a valuable pattern for addressing concurrency challenges and achieving asynchronous execution in software systems. They provide a structured way to encapsulate data and behavior while ensuring safe concurrent access, making them suitable for a wide range of applications, including multi-threaded servers, event-driven systems, and resource management tasks.

6.5 Hiding Implementation Details

Hiding implementation details is a fundamental principle of software design that promotes modularity, encapsulation, and information hiding. This principle suggests that the internal workings of a software component, such as a class or module, should be hidden from external entities, allowing changes to be made to the implementation without affecting the code that relies on the component. This concept is closely related to the idea of abstraction, which allows developers to interact with a component's public interface while ignoring the underlying complexity.

6.5.1 Benefits of Hiding Implementation Details

Hiding implementation details offers several advantages in software development:

1. **Modularity**: By hiding the internal implementation of a component, you create well-defined boundaries between different parts of your system. This modularity makes it easier to manage and maintain the codebase.
2. **Encapsulation**: Hiding implementation details enables encapsulation, which means that the internal state and behavior of a component are not directly accessible from outside. This protects the integrity of the data and allows controlled access through well-defined interfaces.
3. **Abstraction**: Abstraction is the process of simplifying complex systems by modeling them at a higher level of detail. When implementation details are hidden, developers can work with abstract representations of components, making the code more understandable and maintainable.
4. **Ease of Maintenance**: Changes to the internal implementation can be made without affecting external code that relies on the component's public interface. This reduces the risk of introducing bugs when modifying the system.
5. **Flexibility**: Hiding implementation details allows for flexibility in choosing the best implementation for a component. You can optimize and refactor the internal

code as needed without breaking existing code that depends on the component.

6.5.2 Techniques for Hiding Implementation Details

There are several techniques for hiding implementation details in software development:

1. **Encapsulation**: Use access modifiers like private, protected, and public to control the visibility of class members (fields and methods). Private members are only accessible within the class, while public members are accessible from external code.

```python
class MyClass:

def __init__(self):

self.__private_field = 42 # Private field

def public_method(self):

# Public method

print(self.__private_field)
```

1. **Abstraction**: Define abstract classes or interfaces to represent the public contract of a component. Implementations of these contracts can be hidden from external code.

```python
from abc import ABC, abstractmethod

class AbstractComponent(ABC):

@abstractmethod
```

```python
def public_method(self):
```

```python
pass
```

1. **Modules and Packages**: In module-based languages like Python, you can use modules and packages to organize code and hide implementation details. By importing only the necessary modules, you limit exposure to internal code.

```python
# Importing only specific functions or classes from a module
```

```python
from mymodule import public_function
```

1. **Information Hiding**: Avoid exposing internal data structures directly. Instead, provide access to data through methods that encapsulate the behavior and protect the data's integrity.

```python
class Stack:
```

```python
def __init__(self):
```

```python
self.__items = []
```

```python
def push(self, item):
```

```python
self.__items.append(item)
```

```python
def pop(self):
```

```python
if not self.is_empty():
```

```python
return self.__items.pop()
```

```python
else:
```

```python
return None
```

1. **Interfaces and Contracts**: Define clear interfaces and
    contracts that specify the behavior and expectations of
    components. This allows for the decoupling of
    components and the ability to substitute different
    implementations.

```python
from abc import ABC, abstractmethod

class Database(ABC):

@abstractmethod

def connect(self):

pass

@abstractmethod

def query(self, sql):

pass
```

6.5.3 When to Hide Implementation Details

Hiding implementation details is a general principle that should
be applied throughout the software development process. Here are
some specific scenarios where it is especially important:

- **Library and Framework Development**: When
  creating reusable libraries or frameworks, hiding
  implementation details is crucial to provide stable APIs
  while allowing flexibility in the underlying code.

- **API Design**: In the design of APIs, consider what
  should be part of the public interface and what should be

hidden. Providing a clear and concise API while hiding implementation complexity is essential for API users.

• **Large Codebases**: In large codebases with many developers working simultaneously, enforcing the principle of hiding implementation details helps maintain code integrity and reduces the risk of unintended interactions between components.

In conclusion, hiding implementation details is a key principle in software design that promotes modularity, encapsulation, and maintainability. By carefully controlling access to internal code and providing well-defined interfaces, developers can create systems that are easier to understand, maintain, and extend. This practice enhances code robustness and flexibility, ultimately leading to more reliable and efficient software.

Chapter 7: Error Handling

7.1 The Nature of Errors

Error handling is a critical aspect of software development, as no program is immune to errors or unexpected situations. Errors can manifest in various forms, such as bugs, exceptions, or failures, and they can occur at different levels of a software system. Understanding the nature of errors and developing effective error-handling strategies is essential for writing robust and reliable software.

7.1.1 Types of Errors

Errors in software can be categorized into several types:

1. **Compile-Time Errors**: These errors occur during the compilation of the code and prevent the program from being successfully compiled. They are typically related to syntax and type errors. Examples include missing semicolons, undeclared variables, or type mismatches.
2. **Run-Time Errors**: Run-time errors occur while the program is executing. They can result from a wide range of issues, such as invalid input, arithmetic overflows, or null pointer dereferences. Run-time errors can often lead to program crashes or exceptions.
3. **Logical Errors**: Logical errors, also known as bugs, are the most challenging to detect and fix. These errors do not result in immediate crashes but cause the program to produce incorrect or unexpected results. Debugging tools and techniques are essential for identifying and resolving logical errors.
4. **Exceptions**: Exceptions are a form of error handling that

allows a program to gracefully respond to unexpected situations. They can be thrown by the program or raised by external factors, such as input validation failures or file I/O errors.

7.1.2 The Impact of Errors

Errors in software can have significant consequences, depending on the context and severity:

- **Program Crashes**: Run-time errors and unhandled exceptions can lead to program crashes, which can be disruptive and frustrating for users.

- **Data Loss**: Errors during data processing or storage can result in data loss or corruption, which can have serious consequences in applications dealing with sensitive or critical data.

- **Security Vulnerabilities**: Errors in security-related code can lead to security vulnerabilities, such as data breaches or unauthorized access.

- **User Experience**: Bugs and errors can degrade the user experience, leading to user dissatisfaction and a negative perception of the software.

7.1.3 The Importance of Error Handling

Effective error handling is crucial for the following reasons:

1. **Maintaining Stability**: Proper error handling can prevent program crashes and maintain the stability of the software, even in the presence of unexpected errors.

2. **Graceful Degradation**: Error handling allows software to gracefully degrade when errors occur, providing users with informative messages and the ability to recover from errors.
3. **Logging and Debugging**: Error handling mechanisms often include logging, which is essential for diagnosing and debugging issues in production environments.
4. **Security**: Handling errors securely is essential to prevent security vulnerabilities, such as information leakage or denial of service attacks.

7.1.4 Strategies for Error Handling

Effective error handling involves adopting appropriate strategies and techniques, such as:

- **Use of Exceptions**: Exception handling is a powerful mechanism for dealing with errors. It allows you to separate error-handling code from the normal flow of the program and handle errors at different levels of the call stack.

- **Validation**: Input validation is a proactive strategy to prevent errors by ensuring that input data meets expected criteria. Proper validation can reduce the likelihood of errors occurring.

- **Logging**: Logging errors and exceptions provides valuable information for diagnosing issues in production environments. Logging should include details such as error messages, timestamps, and stack traces.

- **Graceful Degradation**: When errors occur, the software should strive to provide meaningful error messages to users and offer options for recovery when possible. Users should not be presented with cryptic error codes.

- **Fail Fast**: In some cases, it may be appropriate to fail fast when detecting certain errors during development or testing. This approach can help identify and address issues early in the development cycle.

Understanding the nature of errors and implementing effective error-handling strategies is essential for building robust and reliable software systems. Error handling should be an integral part of the software development process, from design and implementation to testing and maintenance. By addressing errors proactively, developers can enhance the quality and resilience of their software.

7.2 Error Handling Strategies

Error handling is a critical aspect of software development, and having effective error-handling strategies in place can make a significant difference in the reliability and robustness of a software system. In this section, we'll explore various error-handling strategies and best practices for dealing with errors in your code.

7.2.1 Defensive Programming

Defensive programming is a proactive approach to error handling that focuses on preventing errors before they occur. It involves validating inputs, checking assumptions, and adding safeguards to your code. Here are some key principles of defensive programming:

- **Input Validation**: Always validate user inputs and external data to ensure they meet expected criteria. For example, validate user inputs for data types, ranges, and constraints.

• **Preconditions and Postconditions**: Specify preconditions (conditions that must be met before a function is called) and postconditions (expected outcomes) for functions and methods. This helps prevent invalid usage of functions.

• **Assertions**: Use assertions to express assumptions about the state of your program. Assertions help catch programming errors during development and testing.

• **Fail Fast**: If an error condition is detected, it's often best to fail fast by raising an exception or returning an error code immediately. This prevents the error from propagating and causing further issues.

7.2.2 Exception Handling

Exception handling is a powerful technique for dealing with errors that occur during program execution. It allows you to separate error-handling code from the normal flow of your program. Here are some best practices for exception handling:

• **Use Specific Exceptions**: Create and use specific exception classes that convey meaningful information about the error. Avoid catching general exceptions like Exception unless you have a good reason to do so.

• **Try-Catch Blocks**: Wrap code that may throw exceptions in try-catch blocks. Catch exceptions at the appropriate level of granularity. This allows you to handle different errors differently.

• **Logging**: Always log exceptions, including error messages, timestamps, and stack traces. Logging is invaluable for diagnosing issues in production environments.

• **Resource Management**: Use the try-with-resources (or using in languages like C#) pattern to ensure that resources like files, database connections, or network sockets are properly closed or released.

• **Re-Throwing Exceptions**: When catching exceptions, consider whether it's appropriate to re-throw the exception after logging or handling it. Re-throwing allows higher-level code to handle the error as needed.

7.2.3 Return Values and Error Codes

In addition to exceptions, returning error codes or special values is a common way to signal and handle errors. Here are some practices for using return values and error codes:

• **Consistent Error Codes**: Define a consistent set of error codes or return values for your application. Document their meanings and use them consistently across your codebase.

• **Error Handling Paths**: Clearly define error-handling paths in your code. When a function returns an error code, ensure that calling code checks and handles the error appropriately.

• **Out-Parameters**: If using languages that don't support returning multiple values, consider using out-parameters to return error information alongside the result.

7.2.4 Graceful Degradation

When errors occur, your software should aim to provide a graceful degradation of functionality rather than crashing or producing cryptic error messages. Here are some practices for graceful degradation:

- **User-Friendly Messages**: Present meaningful error messages to users in a language they can understand. Avoid exposing technical details or error codes unless necessary.

- **Fallback Mechanisms**: Implement fallback mechanisms or default values when an error occurs. This allows your software to continue functioning to some extent.

- **Recovery Options**: If possible, offer users recovery options when errors occur. For example, in a document editor, autosave the work when an error prevents manual saving.

7.2.5 Testing and Validation

Testing is a crucial part of error handling. Here are some testing and validation practices:

- **Unit Tests**: Write unit tests that specifically target error conditions. Test not only for expected behavior but also for how your code handles errors.

- **Boundary Testing**: Test edge cases, boundary values, and invalid inputs to ensure your code behaves correctly under different error scenarios.

- **Fuzz Testing**: Use fuzz testing tools and techniques to simulate unexpected inputs and uncover potential vulnerabilities.

- **Code Reviews**: Conduct code reviews with a focus on error handling. Ensure that error-handling code is well-structured and follows best practices.

Effective error handling is a continuous process that involves proactive design, careful coding, rigorous testing, and monitoring in production. By adopting these error-handling strategies and best practices, you can build more reliable and resilient software systems that are better equipped to handle unexpected situations and errors.

7.3 Using Exceptions for Error Handling

Exception handling is a powerful and widely used technique for error handling in many programming languages. It allows you to separate error-handling code from the normal flow of your program, making your code cleaner and more maintainable. In this section, we will delve into using exceptions for error handling and explore best practices.

7.3.1 How Exceptions Work

Exceptions are objects that represent errors or exceptional conditions in your program. When an exceptional condition occurs, an exception is thrown, which means the program jumps to a special block of code designed to handle that exception. This block of code is called a "catch" block.

Here's a basic example in Python:

```
try:
```

 # Code that may raise an exception

result = 10 / 0

except ZeroDivisionError **as** e:

 # Handle the exception

print(f"An error occurred: {e}")

In this example, the code inside the try block attempts to divide 10 by 0, which is not allowed in mathematics. This raises a ZeroDivisionError exception, and the program jumps to the except block, where we handle the exception by printing an error message.

7.3.2 Advantages of Exception Handling

Exception handling offers several advantages for error handling:

- **Separation of Concerns**: Error-handling code is separated from the normal flow of the program, making the code more organized and readable.

- **Multiple Catch Blocks**: You can have multiple catch blocks to handle different types of exceptions separately. This allows you to provide specific error-handling logic for each case.

- **Propagation**: Exceptions can propagate up the call stack until they are caught or until they terminate the program. This means that you can handle exceptions at the appropriate level of your code.

7.3.3 Best Practices for Exception Handling

To make the most of exception handling, consider these best practices:

- **Use Specific Exception Types**: Catch specific exception types rather than catching the generic Exception type. This allows you to handle different error scenarios differently.

- **Catch Only What You Can Handle**: Catch exceptions only if you can handle them effectively. If you can't handle an exception, let it propagate to a higher level where it can be dealt with.

- **Keep Catch Blocks Concise**: Avoid writing lengthy code in catch blocks. Ideally, catch blocks should be concise and focused on error handling. If you need to perform complex operations, consider encapsulating them in separate functions.

- **Logging**: Always log exceptions, including error messages and stack traces. Logging is essential for diagnosing issues in production environments.

- **Resource Cleanup**: If your code allocates resources (like files, database connections, or network sockets), ensure that those resources are properly closed or released in a finally block or using a language-specific construct like using or with.

- **Avoid Swallowing Exceptions**: Be cautious about catching exceptions without taking any action.

Swallowing exceptions (i.e., catching them and not doing anything) can hide issues and make debugging difficult.

• **Rethrowing Exceptions**: In some cases, it's appropriate to rethrow an exception after logging or handling it. This allows higher-level code to handle the error as needed.

• **Custom Exceptions**: Consider creating custom exception classes for specific error scenarios in your application. This can improve the clarity of your code and make it easier to distinguish between different types of exceptions.

7.3.4 Handling Checked vs. Unchecked Exceptions

Some programming languages distinguish between checked exceptions (which must be explicitly caught or declared) and unchecked exceptions (which do not require explicit handling). For example, in Java, exceptions that inherit from RuntimeException are unchecked, while all others are checked.

When dealing with checked exceptions, it's essential to adhere to the language's requirements regarding catching or declaring them. Unchecked exceptions are typically used for severe errors or programming mistakes and may not always be caught explicitly.

7.3.5 Exception Handling in Multithreaded Environments

In multithreaded applications, exception handling can become more complex because exceptions raised in one thread may need to be communicated to other threads. Proper synchronization and coordination mechanisms are essential in such scenarios to ensure that exceptions are handled appropriately.

7.3.6 Using Exception Handling Frameworks

In some languages and frameworks, you may find exception handling libraries or frameworks that provide additional features, such as centralized exception logging, error handling policies, or custom exception types. These can be valuable tools for managing exceptions in large and complex applications.

Exception handling is a fundamental skill in software development. When used correctly, it can make your code more robust and maintainable by allowing you to separate error-handling concerns from the main logic of your program. Understanding how to create, throw, catch, and handle exceptions is essential for writing reliable software that can gracefully handle unexpected situations.

7.4 Wrapping External Dependencies

When developing software, you often need to interact with external dependencies, such as libraries, APIs, databases, or services. Handling errors from these external components is a crucial part of building reliable and robust applications. In this section, we'll explore the concept of wrapping external dependencies to improve error handling.

7.4.1 The Challenges of External Dependencies

External dependencies introduce several challenges related to error handling:

1. **Unpredictable Errors**: External components can fail or behave unexpectedly. They may throw exceptions, return error codes, or provide ambiguous error messages.
2. **Compatibility**: Different external dependencies may have varying error-handling mechanisms, making it challenging

to standardize error handling in your application.

3. **Integration Complexity**: Integrating with external
    dependencies often involves complex interactions and
    multiple failure points, making error handling more
    critical.

7.4.2 Wrapping External Dependencies

To manage errors from external dependencies effectively, it's a common practice to wrap them in a layer of your code. This wrapping involves creating a well-defined interface or API for interacting with the external component while encapsulating its complexities and handling errors consistently.

Here's an example in Python where we wrap a file read operation:

```python
class FileReader:

def __init__(self, file_path):

self.file_path = file_path

def read_file(self):

try:

with open(self.file_path, 'r') as file:

return file.read()

except FileNotFoundError as e:

# Handle the file not found error

print(f"File not found: {e}")

return None
```

except Exception **as** e:

 # Handle other exceptions

print(f"An error occurred while reading the file: {e}")

return None

In this example, the FileReader class wraps the file reading operation. It catches specific exceptions, such as FileNotFoundError, and provides a consistent error-handling interface. If an error occurs, it returns None to indicate an error condition.

7.4.3 Benefits of Wrapping External Dependencies

Wrapping external dependencies offers several advantages:

- **Abstraction**: It abstracts away the complexity of interacting with external components, providing a cleaner and simpler interface for your application code.

- **Consistency**: It enforces consistent error handling for different external dependencies, making your codebase more uniform.

- **Customization**: You can customize error handling to meet your application's specific needs. For example, you can decide how to handle network timeouts or database connection failures.

- **Testing**: Wrappers facilitate easier testing by allowing you to mock or stub external dependencies for unit testing without actually interacting with the external component.

7.4.4 Creating Custom Exception Types

In addition to wrapping external dependencies, it's often beneficial to create custom exception types that represent errors specific to your application. These custom exceptions can provide more meaningful error messages and allow you to distinguish between different error scenarios.

Here's an example in Java of creating a custom exception:

```java
public class CustomDatabaseException extends Exception {

public CustomDatabaseException(String message) {

super(message);

}

}
```

You can then use this custom exception to handle database-related errors in a more tailored manner.

7.4.5 Logging and Monitoring

When handling errors from external dependencies, it's essential to log error details comprehensively. Logging can help you diagnose issues in production and track the performance of external components.

Additionally, consider implementing monitoring and alerting mechanisms to detect and respond to critical errors in real-time. This proactive approach can help minimize downtime and user impact.

7.4.6 Graceful Degradation

When an error occurs in an external dependency, your application should aim for graceful degradation. This means that even if one component fails, the rest of the application should continue to function as smoothly as possible. Implement fallback mechanisms or default behaviors to ensure that your application remains usable despite errors in external dependencies.

7.4.7 Documentation

Proper documentation of error-handling strategies and wrapper classes is crucial for maintaining and scaling your codebase. Document the expected behavior of external dependencies, error handling procedures, and any custom exception types you create.

In summary, wrapping external dependencies and implementing robust error handling is vital for building resilient software applications. It allows you to manage the complexities of external components, maintain consistent error handling, and provide a better user experience by gracefully handling errors. Custom exception types, logging, monitoring, and documentation are essential tools in this process.

7.5 Avoiding Null References

Null references, often represented by null, None, or similar values in different programming languages, can lead to some of the most common and hard-to-debug runtime errors. In this section, we'll explore the concept of avoiding null references and techniques for handling absence of values more safely.

7.5.1 The Problem with Null References

Null references can cause various issues in your code:

1. **NullPointerExceptions**: In languages like Java, dereferencing a null reference leads to a NullPointerException at runtime, potentially crashing your program.
2. **Undefined Behavior**: In some languages, using null references can result in undefined or unexpected behavior, making it challenging to predict the outcome of your code.
3. **Debugging Challenges**: Tracking down the source of null references can be difficult, as they may propagate through multiple levels of function calls.
4. **Code Complexity**: Handling null references often involves defensive programming with numerous null checks, making the code more complex and less readable.

7.5.2 Techniques for Avoiding Null References

To mitigate the problems associated with null references, consider the following techniques:

1. Option Types (Maybe, Option, Nullable)

Option types, also known as Maybe, Option, or Nullable types in different languages, are a functional programming concept that represents the presence or absence of a value explicitly. Instead of returning null, a function can return an option type that either contains a value or is empty.

Here's an example in Kotlin using Nullable:

```kotlin
fun findUserById(id: String): User? {
```

```
// Logic to find user by ID

return userOrNull

}

val user = findUserById("123")

if (user != null) {

// User found, safe to use

} else {

// User not found, handle accordingly

}
```

In this example, the findUserById function returns a nullable User?, making it clear that the result may or may not contain a valid user.

2. Null Object Pattern

The Null Object Pattern involves creating special objects that represent the absence of a value instead of using null references. These objects implement the same interface as the actual objects but provide default or no-op behavior.

```
interface Logger {

void log(String message);

}

class ConsoleLogger implements Logger {

@Override
```

```java
public void log(String message) {

System.out.println(message);

}

}

class NullLogger implements Logger {

@Override

public void log(String message) {

// Do nothing (null behavior)

}

}
```

In this example, we have a NullLogger class that implements the Logger interface but does nothing when log is called. This allows us to avoid null references for logging.

3. Optional Chaining and Safe Navigation Operators

Some programming languages provide optional chaining or safe navigation operators (?. in Kotlin, ?. in C#, ?. in JavaScript). These operators allow you to access properties or call methods on potentially null references without causing a runtime error.

```kotlin
val length = user?.address?.street?.length
```

In this Kotlin example, if any of the properties (user, address, or street) is null, length will be assigned null instead of causing a null reference.ce error.

4. Non-Null Assertions

While it's generally better to avoid null references, there may be situations where you are certain that a reference is non-null at a particular point in your code. In such cases, some languages provide non-null assertions or forced unwrapping mechanisms to indicate your confidence.

// Java

String name = user.getName(); *// Assume user is non-null*

// Kotlin

val name = user!!.name *// Assume user is non-null*

Use non-null assertions sparingly and only when you are absolutely sure about the non-null nature of the reference.

7.5.3 Null Reference Handling Best Practices

To effectively avoid null references and handle absence of values, consider these best practices:

- **Use Option Types**: In languages that support option types, use them to make nullability explicit and handle absence of values safely.

- **Null Object Pattern**: Implement the Null Object Pattern for situations where you need to represent absence of a value with an object.

- **Avoid Returning Null**: In your functions, avoid returning null when a value is not found or an error occurs. Instead, use option types, throw exceptions, or return appropriate default values.

• **Consistent Error Handling**: Use consistent error-handling mechanisms throughout your codebase to handle exceptional cases uniformly.

• **Testing**: Write comprehensive tests to cover scenarios where null references could occur. Use property-based testing or testing frameworks that handle null values effectively.

• **Documentation**: Document your functions and classes to make it clear whether they can return null values. Provide guidance on how to handle null references when necessary.

• **Static Analysis Tools**: Use static code analysis tools that can detect potential null references and provide warnings or suggestions for handling them.

By following these techniques and best practices, you can reduce the risk of null reference-related runtime errors and make your code more reliable and maintainable. Avoiding null references is a crucial step toward writing clean and robust code.

Chapter 8: Boundaries

Boundaries are an integral part of software development, as they define the interaction points between your codebase and external components, such as libraries, frameworks, APIs, or databases. Effective boundary management is essential for creating maintainable and robust software systems. In this chapter, we'll delve into various aspects of working with boundaries and best practices for handling them.

8.1 Working with External Code

External code refers to any code that is not part of your application but is essential for its functionality. This external code can take the form of libraries, frameworks, or third-party APIs. Working with external code presents unique challenges and opportunities, and it's crucial to do so effectively.

8.1.1 Understanding External Dependencies

Before integrating external code into your project, it's essential to have a solid understanding of the dependencies you are introducing. This includes knowing the purpose of the external code, its features, and its potential impact on your project.

Example: Adding a Logging Library

Suppose you want to integrate a logging library into your application. Before doing so, you should research the available logging libraries, consider factors like performance, flexibility, and community support, and assess how well each library aligns with your project's requirements.

8.1.2 Isolation and Decoupling

To maintain clean code, it's advisable to isolate and decouple external code from your application as much as possible. This means encapsulating interactions with external dependencies and minimizing direct dependencies throughout your codebase.

Example: Wrapping External APIs

If your application interacts with a third-party API, consider creating a wrapper or adapter class that encapsulates the API calls. This allows you to manage changes in the external API more effectively and ensures that the rest of your codebase remains relatively unaffected.

```java
public class ExternalApiWrapper {

private ExternalApi externalApi;

public ExternalApiWrapper(ExternalApi externalApi) {

this.externalApi = externalApi;

}

public ApiResponse fetchData() {

// Encapsulate the API call and error handling here

try {

return externalApi.getData();

} catch (ApiException e) {

// Handle API-specific errors
```

```
return new ApiResponse(e.getMessage());

    }

  }

}
```

8.1.3 Dependency Management

Proper dependency management is crucial when working with external code. Use dependency management tools and practices to ensure that your project has the necessary external dependencies, and keep these dependencies up to date to benefit from bug fixes and improvements.

Example: Using Package Managers

Many programming languages have package managers that simplify the process of adding and updating external dependencies. For example, in the JavaScript ecosystem, you can use npm or yarn to manage packages, while in Java, tools like Maven and Gradle handle dependency management.

8.1.4 Testing and Mocking

To maintain code quality and reliability, it's essential to test your application's interactions with external code thoroughly. Use testing frameworks and techniques to create unit tests, integration tests, and even end-to-end tests that verify the correctness of your code when interacting with external dependencies.

Example: Mocking External Services

In unit testing, you can use mocking frameworks to simulate the behavior of external dependencies. For instance, if your code communicates with a web service, you can create mock objects that mimic the service's responses. This allows you to test your code in isolation and verify how it handles different scenarios.

// Using Mockito in Java

ExternalApi mockApi = Mockito.mock(ExternalApi.class);

when(mockApi.getData()).thenReturn(**new** ApiResponse("Mocked Data"));

// Test your code with the mockApi instance

8.1.5 Documentation and Communication

Maintaining clear documentation and communication about the usage of external code is vital for your development team. Document how to integrate, configure, and use external dependencies, and keep your team informed about any changes or updates to these dependencies.

Example: API Documentation

If your application relies on a third-party API, ensure that your team is familiar with the API's documentation. Provide guidelines on authentication, rate limits, error handling, and any best practices recommended by the API provider.

Effective communication and documentation help prevent misunderstandings and ensure that your team can work with external code seamlessly.

In summary, working with external code is a fundamental aspect of software development. Understanding, isolating, and properly managing external dependencies are essential practices for maintaining clean and maintainable code. Effective testing, documentation, and communication are key elements of successful boundary management when dealing with external dependencies.

8.2 Using Third-Party Libraries

In modern software development, third-party libraries play a crucial role in speeding up development, enhancing functionality, and reducing the need to reinvent the wheel. However, using third-party libraries also comes with responsibilities and challenges. In this section, we will explore how to effectively use third-party libraries while maintaining clean code practices.

8.2.1 Choosing the Right Libraries

Selecting the right third-party libraries is a critical decision that can significantly impact your project's success. Consider the following factors when choosing libraries:

1. Purpose and Features

Ensure that the library aligns with the specific needs of your project. Read the library's documentation to understand its features and capabilities. Choose libraries that offer the functionality you require without unnecessary bloat.

2. Community Support and Activity

A thriving and active community is a positive sign for a library. Active communities provide support, bug fixes, and updates. Check for community forums, GitHub repositories, and recent releases to gauge the level of community involvement.

3. Compatibility and Dependencies

Evaluate the library's compatibility with your project's technology stack. Be mindful of the library's dependencies, as they may introduce additional complexity or conflicts with existing dependencies.

4. Licensing

Review the library's licensing terms to ensure they align with your project's licensing requirements. Some libraries may have restrictions or obligations that need to be considered.

5. Maintenance and Longevity

Assess whether the library is actively maintained and whether it has a history of long-term support. Abandoned or unmaintained libraries can become liabilities.

8.2.2 Managing Library Dependencies

Once you've chosen third-party libraries, it's essential to manage their dependencies effectively. Dependency management involves specifying which library versions your project relies on and handling potential conflicts.

Example: Using Dependency Management Tools

Dependency management tools such as npm, yarn (for JavaScript), Maven, Gradle (for Java), and pip (for Python) help you declare and manage library dependencies. These tools simplify the process of adding, updating, and resolving dependencies.

```xml
<!—Maven Example (pom.xml)—>

<dependencies>

<dependency>

<groupId>com.example</groupId>

<artifactId>library-name</artifactId>

<version>1.2.3</version>

</dependency>

</dependencies>
```

8.2.3 Versioning Strategies

Choosing the right library versions and managing them effectively is crucial to prevent compatibility issues and security vulnerabilities. Consider the following versioning strategies:

1. Semantic Versioning (SemVer)

Many libraries follow Semantic Versioning (SemVer), which uses version numbers with three segments: MAJOR.MINOR.PATCH. Adhering to SemVer helps you understand how library updates may impact your project:

- MAJOR version updates may introduce breaking changes.

- MINOR version updates add new features or enhancements.

- PATCH version updates include bug fixes.

2. Lock Files

Some dependency management tools generate lock files (e.g., package-lock.json in npm, yarn.lock in Yarn) that record the exact versions of libraries used in your project. Lock files ensure that your project consistently uses the same library versions across environments.

3. Dependency Auditing

Regularly audit your project's dependencies for security vulnerabilities. Many tools and services can analyze your project's dependencies and alert you to known vulnerabilities.

8.2.4 Code Quality and Third-Party Code

When using third-party libraries, it's essential to maintain code quality within your project. This includes following clean code practices, adhering to coding standards, and ensuring that your code integrates seamlessly with the libraries.

Example: Wrapping Third-Party Libraries

To isolate your code from the specifics of a third-party library and maintain clean code, consider creating wrapper classes or adapters. These wrappers encapsulate the library's functionality and provide a clean and consistent interface for your codebase.

```java
// Example in Java with a database library

public class DatabaseService {

private ThirdPartyDatabaseLibrary database;

public DatabaseService(ThirdPartyDatabaseLibrary database) {

this.database = database;

}

public void saveData(String key, String value) {

// Encapsulate the library-specific code here

database.save(key, value);

}

}
```

8.2.5 Documentation and Training

Ensure that your team is well-informed about the third-party libraries you use. Provide documentation or training sessions to explain how to use the libraries correctly and efficiently. Encourage team members to read the library's official documentation and stay updated on changes.

8.2.6 Monitoring and Updates

Stay vigilant about library updates and changes. Subscribe to release notes and security advisories for the libraries you use. Regularly update your project's dependencies to benefit from bug fixes, performance improvements, and security patches.

In conclusion, third-party libraries are valuable assets in software development, but their effective use requires careful consideration and management. Choose libraries wisely, manage dependencies meticulously, adhere to versioning strategies, maintain code

8.3 Wrapping External APIs

When working on a software project, you often need to interact with external services, databases, or APIs. These interactions introduce boundaries between your code and the external world. To maintain clean code, it's essential to encapsulate these interactions effectively. In this section, we'll explore the concept of wrapping external APIs and how it can improve code quality and maintainability.

8.3.1 The Need for Wrapping

External APIs, such as web services, databases, or third-party libraries, come with their own complexities and dependencies. Directly embedding calls to these APIs throughout your codebase can lead to several problems:

1. Tight Coupling

Direct calls to external APIs tightly couple your code to the implementation details of those APIs. This makes your code less flexible and harder to maintain, as any changes to the external API can have widespread impacts on your code.

2. Testability

Testing code that directly interacts with external APIs can be challenging. External APIs may have unpredictable behaviors or require expensive setup, making it difficult to write unit tests for your code.

3. Code Readability

Code that directly includes API calls can become cluttered and less readable. Understanding the core logic of your application becomes difficult when interspersed with low-level API interactions.

Example: Direct API Call

```python
# Direct API call without wrapping

def fetch_user_data(user_id):

    response = requests.get(f"https://api.example.com/users/{user_id}")

    if response.status_code == 200:

        return response.json()

    else:

        raise Exception("Failed to fetch user data")
```

8.3.2 Wrapping External APIs

To address these issues, it's advisable to wrap external APIs within your codebase. Wrapping involves creating intermediary components or classes that abstract the interaction with the external API. These wrappers provide a clean and consistent interface for your code to interact with the external service.

Example: Wrapping an API Call

 # Wrapping the API call in a service class

class UserService:

def __init__(self, base_url):

self.base_url = base_url

def fetch_user_data(self, user_id):

response = requests.get(f"{self.base_url}/users/{user_id}")

if response.status_code == 200:

return response.json()

else:

raise Exception("Failed to fetch user data")

By wrapping the external API call in a UserService class, we isolate the API interaction, making it more maintainable and testable. Additionally, this approach allows us to change the underlying API implementation or replace it with minimal impact on the rest of the codebase.

8.3.3 Benefits of Wrapping

Wrapping external APIs offers several advantages:

1. Decoupling

Wrapping reduces the coupling between your code and external services. If the external service changes or needs to be replaced, you only need to update the wrapper, minimizing the impact on the rest of your code.

2. Testability

With wrapped APIs, you can easily mock or stub the external service during testing. This enables you to write unit tests for your code without relying on the actual external service, improving test coverage and reliability.

3. Encapsulation

Wrappers encapsulate the complexities of external APIs, providing a clear and concise interface for your code. This makes your codebase more readable and easier to understand for both new and existing team members.

4. Consistency

A well-designed wrapper enforces consistent usage patterns for interacting with external services. This consistency can prevent common errors and improve code quality.

8.3.4 Design Considerations

When wrapping external APIs, consider the following design principles:

1. Separation of Concerns

Design your wrappers to adhere to the separation of concerns principle. Each wrapper should have a specific responsibility related to the external API it encapsulates. Avoid creating monolithic wrapper classes that handle multiple, unrelated tasks.

2. Abstraction

Abstract away the low-level details of the external API. Your wrapper should provide a higher-level interface that shields your code from the intricacies of the external service.

3. Error Handling

Handle errors and exceptions gracefully within the wrappers. Clearly define error handling strategies and ensure that errors from the external service are translated into meaningful exceptions or error codes in your codebase.

4. Documentation

Document your wrappers thoroughly. Include clear descriptions of how to use the wrappers, the expected inputs and outputs, and any error scenarios. Well-documented wrappers make it easier for other developers to work with your code.

In conclusion, wrapping external APIs is a valuable practice for clean code development. It promotes decoupling, testability, encapsulation, and consistency. When designing wrappers, adhere to separation of concerns, abstraction, error handling, and documentation best practices to ensure that your code remains clean and maintainable while interacting with external services.

8.4 Learning Boundaries Through Tests

In software development, understanding and interacting with external boundaries such as databases, web services, and third-party libraries is a common and crucial task. These boundaries are often points of interaction where your code communicates with external systems. Learning how to work with boundaries effectively can lead to cleaner, more maintainable code. One valuable approach to gaining confidence and understanding about boundaries is through testing.

8.4.1 The Challenges of Boundary Interaction

Boundary interactions can be challenging for several reasons:

1. External Dependencies

External systems have their own dependencies, requirements, and potential for failure. Dealing with these dependencies can introduce complexity into your code.

2. Unpredictable Behavior

External systems may behave unpredictably, with various responses and error conditions. Understanding and handling these behaviors is critical.

3. Integration Complexity

Integrating with external systems often involves complex interactions, including authentication, data transformation, and error handling. Ensuring your code handles these complexities correctly is essential.

8.4.2 Writing Tests for Boundary Interactions

Writing tests that exercise boundary interactions can help mitigate these challenges and provide the following benefits:

1. Learning and Documentation

Tests that interact with external boundaries serve as documentation for how your code interacts with external systems. They provide a clear picture of the expected behavior and requirements.

2. Isolation

Tests can isolate the boundary interaction code from the rest of your application. This allows you to focus on testing the specific behavior related to the boundary and ensures that changes in other parts of your codebase do not affect these interactions.

3. Reproducibility

Tests provide a reproducible way to verify that your code behaves correctly when interacting with external systems. This is particularly valuable when you need to detect and debug issues.

Example: Testing a Database Boundary

```python
import unittest

from myapp.database import DatabaseConnection

class TestDatabaseInteraction(unittest.TestCase):

    def test_fetch_user_data(self):
```

```
# Create a test database connection

db_connection = DatabaseConnection("test_database")

# Insert test data

db_connection.execute("INSERT INTO users (id, name) VALUES
(1, 'Alice')")

# Fetch user data

user_data = db_connection.fetch_user_data(1)

# Verify the expected user data

self.assertEqual(user_data["id"], 1)

self.assertEqual(user_data["name"], "Alice")
```

In this example, we have a test case that exercises the boundary interaction with a database. We create a test database connection, insert test data, and then fetch and verify user data. This test ensures that our code interacts correctly with the database boundary.

8.4.3 Strategies for Boundary Tests

When writing tests for boundary interactions, consider the following strategies:

1. Mocking and Stubbing

Use mocking or stubbing to isolate the boundary interaction from external dependencies. Mocking allows you to create controlled, predictable responses from external systems without actually making real requests or connections.

2. *End-to-End Tests*

In addition to unit tests that mock boundaries, consider end-to-end tests that exercise real interactions with external systems. These tests provide a higher level of confidence but may be slower and more complex to set up.

3. *Error Scenarios*

Include tests that cover error scenarios, such as network failures, timeouts, or unexpected responses from external systems. Ensuring that your code handles these situations gracefully is crucial.

4. *Test Data Management*

Effectively manage test data for external systems. Consider using dedicated test environments or resetting data between tests to maintain a clean state.

5. *Documentation*

Use descriptive test names and comments to document the purpose and behavior of your boundary tests. This documentation helps other developers understand how your code interacts with external systems.

8.4.4 Continuous Learning

Gaining confidence and proficiency in working with external boundaries is an ongoing process. As your codebase evolves and integrates with new systems, continue to write and maintain boundary tests to ensure that your interactions remain clean, reliable, and well-documented.

In conclusion, writing tests for boundary interactions is a valuable practice for clean code development. It helps you understand, document, and isolate interactions with external systems, improving the reliability and maintainability of your code. Use mocking, end-to-end tests, error scenarios, and effective test data management to create comprehensive tests that cover various aspects of boundary interactions.

8.5 Decoupling from Frameworks

Decoupling your code from external frameworks and libraries is a fundamental principle of clean code. While frameworks and libraries provide powerful tools and functionality, tightly coupling your code to them can lead to several problems, including reduced flexibility, increased complexity, and decreased maintainability. In this section, we'll explore the importance of decoupling from frameworks and techniques to achieve it.

8.5.1 The Dangers of Tight Coupling

Tight coupling occurs when your code becomes dependent on specific features, interfaces, or behaviors of an external framework or library. This can have several negative consequences:

1. Reduced Flexibility

Tightly coupled code is less flexible and adaptable to changes. If the framework or library evolves or needs to be replaced, your code may require extensive modifications.

2. Increased Complexity

Coupled code tends to be more complex because it must accommodate the intricacies of the framework. This complexity can make your code harder to understand and maintain.

3. Difficulty in Testing

Testing tightly coupled code can be challenging. You may need to set up the entire framework or rely on complex mocking, which can lead to slow and brittle tests.

4. Vendor Lock-In

Tight coupling with a specific framework can result in vendor lock-in, making it difficult to switch to alternative solutions or platforms.

8.5.2 Techniques for Decoupling

To decouple your code from frameworks and libraries, consider the following techniques:

1. Abstraction and Interfaces

Create abstractions and interfaces that define the interactions with the framework or library. Your code can then depend on these abstractions rather than specific implementation details.

```python
# Bad: Tight coupling to a specific database library

import specific_db_library

def fetch_data():
```

```python
connection = specific_db_library.connect("my_database")

result = connection.query("SELECT * FROM data")

# ...

# Good: Decoupled using an interface

class DatabaseInterface:

def connect(self, database_name):

pass

def query(self, query):

pass

def fetch_data(database: DatabaseInterface):

connection = database.connect("my_database")

result = database.query("SELECT * FROM data")

# ...
```

2. Dependency Injection

Use dependency injection to provide framework-related dependencies to your code rather than hard-coding them. This allows you to switch implementations or use mock objects during testing.

```python
# Bad: Hard-coded dependency on a specific email service

import specific_email_service

def send_email(message):
```

```python
service = specific_email_service.EmailService()

service.send(message)

# ...

# Good: Dependency injection

class EmailServiceInterface:

def send(self, message):

pass

def send_email(service: EmailServiceInterface, message):

service.send(message)

# ...
```

3. Adapter Pattern

If you must integrate with a framework, consider using the Adapter pattern to encapsulate the framework-specific code and provide a clean interface to your application code.

4. Dependency Inversion Principle (DIP)

Follow the Dependency Inversion Principle, which suggests that high-level modules (your application code) should not depend on low-level modules (frameworks or libraries). Both should depend on abstractions.

8.5.3 Benefits of Decoupling

Decoupling your code from frameworks offers several advantages:

1. Improved Testability

Decoupled code is easier to test because you can replace framework dependencies with mock objects or stubs, allowing you to write unit tests more effectively.

2. Greater Flexibility

Your code becomes more adaptable to changes in frameworks or the introduction of new ones. It can also be reused in different contexts.

3. Enhanced Maintainability

Code that is decoupled from frameworks is typically cleaner and easier to maintain. It's easier to understand, modify, and debug.

4. Reduced Vendor Lock-In

Decoupled code is less likely to be locked into a specific framework or library, giving you the freedom to switch or upgrade as needed.

In conclusion, decoupling your code from external frameworks and libraries is essential for clean code development. It improves flexibility, reduces complexity, enhances testability, and promotes maintainability. Use techniques such as abstraction, interfaces, dependency injection, and the Adapter pattern to achieve decoupling while following the Dependency Inversion Principle. This practice will lead to more robust and adaptable software systems.

Chapter 9: Unit Tests

9.1 The Role of Unit Tests in Clean Code

Unit tests are an integral part of clean code development. They serve as a crucial tool for ensuring the correctness, maintainability, and robustness of your codebase. In this section, we'll explore the role of unit tests in clean code and discuss why they are essential.

What Are Unit Tests?

Unit tests are small, focused tests that validate the behavior of individual components or units of code, typically functions or methods. These tests aim to answer the question, "Does this piece of code work as expected?" By isolating and testing specific units of code in isolation, you can catch defects early in the development process.

The Benefits of Unit Tests

Unit tests provide several important benefits when it comes to writing clean code:

1. Verification of Correctness: Unit tests verify that your code behaves as intended. When you write a unit test, you explicitly define the expected behavior of a piece of code. If the code's behavior changes in the future due to changes elsewhere in the codebase, the unit test will fail, alerting you to potential issues.

2. Documentation: Well-written unit tests serve as documentation for your code. They provide examples of how to use the code and can help other developers understand its intended behavior.

3. Maintainability: Unit tests make it easier to refactor your code with confidence. When you make changes, you can run the unit tests to ensure that existing functionality still works as expected. If a test fails, you know you've introduced a regression, and you can fix it before it becomes a larger problem.

4. Regression Prevention: Unit tests act as a safety net to catch regressions. When you add new features or fix bugs, running the existing unit tests ensures that you haven't inadvertently broken existing functionality.

5. Improved Design: Writing unit tests often encourages you to write code with better design. Code that is difficult to test is often a sign of poor architecture or tight coupling, pushing you to refactor and improve the code's structure.

Test-Driven Development (TDD)

One approach to writing unit tests is Test-Driven Development (TDD). In TDD, you write tests before you write the actual code. This practice helps you think deeply about the desired behavior of your code before implementation. The TDD cycle typically consists of three steps:

1. Write a failing unit test that defines the behavior you want to implement.
2. Write the minimum amount of code necessary to make the test pass.
3. Refactor the code if needed, ensuring it meets the desired design principles and remains clean.

TDD is a powerful technique for producing clean code with high test coverage. It promotes a test-first mindset and encourages incremental development.

Conclusion

Unit tests play a vital role in clean code development. They serve as a safety net, documentation, and design tool. By writing unit tests, following TDD practices, and ensuring high test coverage, you can create code that is more reliable, maintainable, and adaptable to change. In the following sections, we'll delve deeper into the principles of writing clean tests and explore various aspects of unit testing.

9.2 Writing Clean Tests

Writing clean tests is as important as writing clean code. Clean tests are easy to read, understand, and maintain, and they provide confidence in the correctness of your code. In this section, we'll explore the principles and practices that contribute to writing clean tests.

9.2.1 The Characteristics of Clean Tests

Clean tests exhibit several key characteristics:

1. Readability: Clean tests are easy to read and understand.

Anyone, including team members and future maintainers, should be able to comprehend the purpose and expected behavior of a test without extensive effort.

2. Isolation: Tests should be isolated from one another. Each test should run independently and not rely on the state or setup of other tests. This ensures that a failing test doesn't impact the execution of subsequent tests.

3. Consistency: Follow consistent naming conventions and structure for your test cases. Consistency makes it easier to locate and understand tests, especially in larger codebases.

4. Clarity: Test cases should be clear and self-explanatory. Use descriptive names for test methods and variables. Avoid overly complex or convoluted test logic.

5. Minimal Setup: Keep test setup minimal. If a test requires complex setup or extensive configuration, it can make the test harder to understand and maintain. Aim for simplicity.

6. Robustness: Tests should be robust against changes in the code they are testing. A change in the implementation of the code being tested should ideally require minimal or no changes to the corresponding test.

7. Fast Execution: Tests should execute quickly. Slow tests can hinder the development workflow, especially when running tests frequently during development.

9.2.2 Tips for Writing Clean Tests

To write clean tests, consider the following tips:

1. Use Descriptive Test Names: Choose descriptive names for your test methods that clearly indicate the scenario being tested and the expected outcome. A well-named test is a form of documentation.

2. One Assertion Per Test: Aim to have one logical assertion per test. This keeps your tests focused and makes it clear what aspect of the code you are testing.

3. Avoid Magic Values: Avoid hardcoding values in your tests, especially magic values. Use constants or variables with meaningful names to make your test cases more understandable.

```python
# Bad: Magic value in a test

def test_calculate_total():

result = calculate_total(5, 3)

assert result == 8 # What does 8 represent?

# Good: Using constants

def test_calculate_total():

price = 5

quantity = 3

result = calculate_total(price, quantity)

assert result == price * quantity
```

4. Arrange-Act-Assert (AAA) Pattern: Structure your test methods using the AAA pattern. Arrange sets up the test, Act performs the action being tested, and Assert verifies the expected outcome.

```python
def test_addition():

# Arrange

x = 5

y = 3

# Act

result = add(x, y)

# Assert

assert result == 8
```

5. Keep Tests Short and Focused: Avoid long and complex test methods. If a test method becomes too lengthy, consider refactoring it into multiple smaller tests, each focusing on a specific aspect of the functionality.

6. Use Test Data Builders: For tests that require complex object creation, consider using test data builders to simplify setup and improve test readability.

```python
# Without a test data builder

user = User(name="Alice", email="alice@example.com", age=30)

# With a test data builder
```

```
user                                                          =
UserDataBuilder().with_name("Alice").with_email("alice@example.com").w
```

7. Avoid Conditional Logic in Tests: Minimize conditional logic within test methods. Conditional logic can make tests harder to understand and maintain. If multiple test cases are needed to cover different conditions, consider writing separate test methods for each case.

```python
# Bad: Conditional logic in a test

def test_discount_calculation():

if is_vip_customer:

discount = calculate_vip_discount(total)

else:

discount = calculate_regular_discount(total)

assert discount == expected_discount

# Better: Separate test methods

def test_vip_customer_discount():

discount = calculate_vip_discount(total)

assert discount == expected_discount

def test_regular_customer_discount():

discount = calculate_regular_discount(total)

assert discount == expected_discount
```

8. Use Setup and Teardown Appropriately: Use setup and teardown methods provided by your testing framework to set up and clean up test-specific resources. This helps maintain test isolation.

9.2.3 Clean Test Code Example

Here's an example of a clean test:

```
def test_calculate_total_with_discount():
    # Arrange
    price = 10
    quantity = 5
    customer = Customer(is_vip=True)
    # Act
    total = calculate_total(price, quantity, customer)
    # Assert
    assert total == 45 # 10 * 5 with a VIP discount
```

This test follows the AAA pattern, has

9.3 Testing Private Methods

In the realm of unit testing, the question of whether to test private methods often arises. Private methods, as the name suggests, are intended to be hidden from external access, and the primary focus of unit tests is to verify the behavior of public methods. However, there are situations where testing private methods can be beneficial, and there are strategies to approach this.

9.3.1 The Case for Testing Private Methods

1. Complex Private Logic: Sometimes, a private method may contain complex logic that plays a crucial role in the behavior of the class. In such cases, it can be valuable to have unit tests that specifically target and validate this logic. It can provide a safety net for refactoring and prevent regressions.

2. Private Methods with Side Effects: If a private method has side effects that indirectly affect the class's public behavior, it may be worth testing. Verifying these side effects can be essential for ensuring the correctness of the class.

3. Legacy Code: In legacy codebases, where public methods are tightly coupled to private methods, it might be challenging to write tests for the public methods without also indirectly testing the private methods. In such situations, testing private methods can be a pragmatic approach to improve test coverage.

9.3.2 Strategies for Testing Private Methods

Testing private methods can be challenging, as they are not meant to be directly accessible from test code. However, there are several strategies to work around this limitation:

1. Reflection: Some programming languages and testing frameworks allow you to use reflection to access and invoke private methods. While this can be a powerful technique, it should be used with caution, as it can make tests brittle and tightly coupled to the implementation.

 # Python example using reflection

```
def test_private_method():

obj = MyClass()

private_method = obj._MyClass__private_method # Access private
method using name mangling

result = private_method()

assert result == expected_result
```

2. Protected or Package-Private Methods: If the language allows it, you can make the method protected or package-private (accessible within the same package or module). This makes it technically accessible for testing while still discouraging external use.

3. Extract Private Logic: Consider refactoring private methods with complex logic into separate classes or functions that are public and can be tested independently. This promotes better separation of concerns and testability.

4. Use White-Box Testing: In white-box testing, you focus on testing the behavior of the class, including its private methods, by examining the code's internal structure. Tools like code coverage analysis can help identify untested code paths.

9.3.3 Guidelines for Testing Private Methods

If you decide to test private methods, keep these guidelines in mind:

1. Test Behavior, Not Implementation: When testing private methods, focus on the expected behavior rather than the internal implementation details. Testing implementation details can make tests fragile and less maintainable.

2. Avoid Overly Granular Tests: Avoid writing overly granular tests that test every tiny aspect of a private method. Instead, aim for tests that cover meaningful scenarios and ensure the method behaves correctly in different contexts.

3. Refactor When Necessary: If you find that you need to test private methods frequently, it might indicate design issues. Consider refactoring the class to have clearer public interfaces and move complex logic to separate components.

4. Maintain a Balance: Strive for a balance between testing private methods and testing the class's public behavior. Overreliance on testing private methods can lead to brittle tests and hinder code maintainability.

In conclusion, while the primary focus of unit testing is on public methods, there are scenarios where testing private methods can be beneficial. However, it should be approached cautiously, and the emphasis should always be on testing behavior rather than implementation details. Testing private methods should be a means to an end, not the end goal of unit testing.

9.4 The Three Laws of TDD (Test-Driven Development)

Test-Driven Development (TDD) is a software development approach that places a strong emphasis on writing tests before writing the actual code. It follows a simple and iterative cycle often described as the "Three Laws of TDD." These laws guide the developer through the process of writing clean, maintainable code with high test coverage.

9.4.1 The First Law: You Must Write a Failing Test Before You Write Production Code

The first law of TDD is simple but foundational. It dictates that before you write any production code, you must first write a failing test. This test should capture a specific behavior or requirement that your code must satisfy. Writing a failing test means that you are beginning with a clear expectation of what you want to achieve.

The benefits of this law are profound:

- **Clarity of Intent:** It forces you to define the desired behavior of your code upfront, making your intent explicit.

- **Measurable Progress:** You can measure your progress based on the number of failing tests. As you write production code, your goal is to make these tests pass one by one.

- **Prevention of Over-Engineering:** You avoid the common pitfall of over-engineering a solution before understanding the problem fully. By starting with a failing test, you stay focused on solving the immediate problem.

9.4.2 The Second Law: You Must Write Only Enough Production Code to Make the Test Pass

The second law complements the first by guiding how much production code you should write in response to a failing test. It emphasizes that you should write just enough code to make the test pass—no more and no less. This law encourages simplicity and minimalism in your code.

By adhering to the second law, you achieve several benefits:

- **Simplicity:** Your code remains simple and focused on solving the immediate problem, avoiding unnecessary complexity.

- **Continuous Progress:** You make incremental progress with each passing test, reducing the chances of getting stuck on a complex problem.

- **Maintainability:** With minimal code changes, it's easier to maintain and refactor your code later.

9.4.3 The Third Law: You Must Refactor Only After Writing a Passing Test

The third law underscores the importance of refactoring. It states that you should refactor your code only after you have a passing test. This is a crucial step in keeping your codebase clean and maintainable.

Refactoring involves improving the structure, design, and readability of your code without changing its behavior. By refactoring after each passing test, you ensure that your codebase remains clean and that any technical debt is addressed promptly.

The benefits of the third law include:

- **Continuous Improvement:** You iteratively improve your codebase, ensuring that it evolves in a controlled and sustainable manner.

- **Maintainability:** Regular refactoring prevents the accumulation of technical debt, making your code easier to maintain over time.

- **Flexibility:** You can confidently make changes to your code in response to changing requirements because you have a comprehensive suite of tests to catch regressions.

In conclusion, the Three Laws of TDD provide a structured approach to software development that emphasizes testing, simplicity, and maintainability. By following these laws, developers can create robust and clean code while ensuring that it remains adaptable to changing needs. TDD is not only a testing technique but a design and development philosophy that leads to higher code quality.

9.5 The Clean Test Mindset

Writing unit tests is a fundamental practice in software development, and adopting a clean test mindset can significantly impact the quality of your codebase. A clean test mindset means approaching the creation of tests with the same care and discipline as writing production code. In this section, we'll explore the principles and practices that constitute a clean test mindset.

9.5.1 Clarity and Readability

Just as with production code, the clarity and readability of your tests are paramount. Clean tests should be easy to understand, even for someone who is not familiar with the specifics of the code being tested. Consider the following practices to enhance clarity and readability:

- **Descriptive Test Names:** Choose descriptive and meaningful names for your test methods. A well-named test method should convey the scenario being tested.

- **Structured Test Cases:** Organize your test cases in a structured and consistent manner. This can involve arranging your tests in a logical order and grouping related tests.

- **Minimal Test Logic:** Keep the logic within your test methods minimal. Tests should primarily consist of arranging the test scenario, performing an action, and asserting the expected outcomes.

9.5.2 Isolation and Independence

Clean tests should be isolated and independent of each other. Each test should execute in isolation, without depending on the state or side effects of other tests. Achieving isolation and independence is crucial for the reliability of your test suite:

- **Arrange-Act-Assert (AAA) Pattern:** Follow the AAA pattern, which separates the arrangement of test data, the execution of the test action, and the assertion of results. This pattern helps maintain test isolation.

- **Avoid Shared State:** Avoid sharing state, resources, or data between tests. Tests that rely on shared state can become fragile and hard to maintain.

9.5.3 Maintainability and Refactoring

Just like production code, tests need maintenance and occasional refactoring. A clean test mindset includes practices that support the long-term maintainability of your test suite:

- **Regular Review:** Review and refactor your tests regularly. Eliminate redundant or obsolete tests and improve the clarity of existing ones.

- **Feedback-Driven Improvement:** Act on feedback from test failures. When a test fails, consider whether the test or the production code needs adjustment.

- **Keep Tests DRY:** Apply the "Don't Repeat Yourself" (DRY) principle to your tests. If you find duplicated test code, consider extracting it into helper methods or shared fixtures.

9.5.4 Coverage and Completeness

A clean test mindset also emphasizes test coverage and completeness. Aim to cover different scenarios, edge cases, and potential sources of errors in your code:

- **Boundary and Edge Cases:** Design tests that explore boundary conditions and edge cases. These are often where bugs lurk.

- **Happy and Sad Paths:** Test both the expected (happy path) and unexpected (sad path) behavior of your code. Ensure that error-handling paths are adequately tested.

- **Branches and Conditions:** Ensure that your tests cover different branches and conditional logic in your code. This helps catch logic errors.

9.5.5 Automation and Continuous Integration

Automation is a cornerstone of a clean test mindset. Automated tests can be run frequently, providing rapid feedback to developers:

- **Continuous Integration (CI):** Integrate your tests into a CI pipeline. This ensures that tests are automatically executed whenever changes are made to the codebase, helping catch regressions early.

- **Fast and Isolated:** Write tests that are fast to execute and can run in isolation. Slow tests can discourage developers from running them frequently.

In summary, adopting a clean test mindset is essential for maintaining a robust and reliable codebase. Clean tests are clear, isolated, maintainable, cover relevant scenarios, and are automated for continuous feedback. By applying these principles and practices, you can ensure that your test suite remains a valuable asset throughout the software development lifecycle.

Chapter 10: Classes

10.1 Class Design Principles

In the previous chapters, we have explored various aspects of clean code, including meaningful names, functions, and the organization of code at different scales. Now, let's delve into the principles of designing classes that adhere to clean code practices. Well-designed classes are the building blocks of a clean and maintainable codebase.

The Significance of Class Design

Classes play a central role in object-oriented programming (OOP). They serve as blueprints for creating objects, encapsulating both data and behavior. Effective class design is essential for several reasons:

1. **Abstraction:** Classes allow you to abstract away complex implementation details, exposing only the necessary interface to the outside world. This abstraction simplifies code consumption.
2. **Modularity:** Well-designed classes promote modularity by encapsulating related functionality into self-contained units. This modularity enhances code organization and reusability.
3. **Maintainability:** Clean class design makes your codebase more maintainable. When classes have clear responsibilities and follow established design principles, it becomes easier to make changes without causing unintended side effects.

SOLID Principles

To achieve clean class design, you can follow the SOLID principles, which are a set of five object-oriented design principles:

1. **Single Responsibility Principle (SRP):** A class should have only one reason to change. It should have a single responsibility or job. When a class has multiple responsibilities, it becomes fragile and challenging to maintain.

2. **Open-Closed Principle (OCP):** Software entities (classes, modules, functions) should be open for extension but closed for modification. This means you can extend their behavior without altering their source code.

3. **Liskov Substitution Principle (LSP):** Subtypes must be substitutable for their base types without altering the correctness of the program. In other words, derived classes should adhere to the contract established by their base classes.

4. **Interface Segregation Principle (ISP):** Clients should not be forced to depend on interfaces they do not use. This principle encourages the creation of small, focused interfaces tailored to specific client needs.

5. **Dependency Inversion Principle (DIP):** High-level modules should not depend on low-level modules. Both should depend on abstractions. Abstractions should not depend on details; details should depend on abstractions. This principle promotes loose coupling between classes.

Cohesion and Coupling

In addition to the SOLID principles, consider the concepts of cohesion and coupling when designing classes:

- **Cohesion:** High cohesion implies that a class has a single, well-defined purpose. Cohesive classes are focused and do not try to do too much. Aim for high cohesion within your classes.

- **Coupling:** Low coupling indicates that classes are loosely connected and have minimal dependencies on each other. Reducing coupling between classes improves code maintainability and flexibility.

Class Size and Complexity

The size and complexity of a class matter when it comes to clean code. Ideally, classes should be small and focused. Large classes with many methods and properties tend to become unwieldy and harder to maintain.

Consider breaking down large classes into smaller ones, each with a specific responsibility. This not only improves code organization but also allows for better reuse of individual components.

Inheritance and Composition

When designing classes, favor composition over inheritance. Inheritance can lead to tight coupling and make code more challenging to change. Composition allows you to combine and reuse components more flexibly.

Additionally, when inheritance is used, ensure that it adheres to the Liskov Substitution Principle (LSP) to prevent unexpected behavior in derived classes.

Design for Change

Lastly, design your classes with change in mind. Anticipate future requirements and design classes to be extensible. Following SOLID principles and considering class size, cohesion, and coupling will make your codebase more adaptable to change.

In the upcoming sections of this chapter, we will delve deeper into these class design principles and provide practical examples of applying them to create clean and maintainable classes.

10.2 Keeping Classes Small and Focused

In the previous section, we discussed the importance of adhering to the Single Responsibility Principle (SRP) as one of the SOLID principles when designing classes. SRP states that a class should have only one reason to change, which means it should have a single, well-defined responsibility. To follow this principle effectively, it's essential to keep your classes small and focused.

The Problems of Large Classes

Large classes can lead to several problems in your codebase:

1. **Complexity:** Large classes tend to be more complex, making it challenging to understand and maintain them. As the class grows, so does the cognitive load required to work with it.
2. **Maintenance Difficulty:** When a class has multiple responsibilities, any change to one of those responsibilities can affect the entire class. This can lead to unintended side effects and make maintenance more error-prone.
3. **Testing Complexity:** Testing large classes can be difficult, as you need to cover all possible code paths within a single unit test. This increases the effort required for thorough testing.
4. **Reusability:** Large classes are often less reusable because they are tightly coupled to specific functionalities. Smaller classes with well-defined responsibilities are more likely to be reusable in various contexts.

Strategies for Keeping Classes Small

To keep your classes small and focused, consider the following strategies:

1. **Single Responsibility:** Ensure that each class has a clear and single responsibility. If you find that a class is responsible for multiple tasks, consider refactoring it into smaller, more focused classes.
2. **Divide and Conquer:** Break down large classes into smaller ones based on their responsibilities. This division should result in classes that are easier to understand, test, and maintain.
3. **Use Composition:** Instead of adding more methods and properties to a class, consider using composition to encapsulate related functionality in separate objects. This promotes modularity and smaller class sizes.
4. **Extract Methods:** If a method within a class becomes too long or complex, extract portions of it into separate methods. This not only improves readability but also allows you to reuse those extracted methods if needed.
5. **Apply Design Patterns:** Familiarize yourself with common design patterns like the Factory Pattern, Singleton Pattern, and Strategy Pattern. These patterns often lead to smaller, more focused classes with specific responsibilities.

Benefits of Small and Focused Classes

Maintaining small and focused classes offers several benefits:

- **Readability:** Smaller classes are easier to read and understand, leading to better code comprehension for both developers and maintainers.

- **Testability:** Smaller classes are more straightforward to test, as you can focus on testing individual behaviors without the complexity of large, multifaceted classes.

- **Reusability:** Small classes with well-defined responsibilities are more reusable in different parts of your application or in future projects.

- **Scalability:** As your codebase grows, small classes are easier to scale and adapt to new requirements, reducing the likelihood of code becoming unwieldy.

In summary, the size and focus of your classes play a crucial role in maintaining clean and maintainable code. By adhering to the Single Responsibility Principle and employing strategies to keep classes small, you can improve code readability, testability, reusability, and scalability while reducing complexity and maintenance challenges.

10.3 Single Responsibility Principle (SRP)

The Single Responsibility Principle (SRP) is one of the SOLID principles of object-oriented design. It states that a class should have only one reason to change, meaning it should have a single, well-defined responsibility. SRP is a fundamental principle in clean code development because it promotes code that is easier to understand, maintain, and extend.

Understanding the SRP

The SRP can be summarized in a simple statement: "A class should have only one reason to change." This means that a class should encapsulate a single responsibility, and any changes to that responsibility should result in changes to that class and no other. When a class has multiple responsibilities, it becomes tightly coupled to various parts of the system, making it more challenging to modify and maintain.

Benefits of SRP

Adhering to SRP offers several advantages in software development:

1. **Easier Maintenance:** When a class has a single responsibility, changes related to that responsibility are isolated. This makes it easier to locate and modify the relevant code, reducing the risk of introducing unintended side effects.
2. **Enhanced Testability:** Classes with well-defined responsibilities are typically easier to test because you can focus on testing specific behaviors. This promotes more thorough testing and early detection of issues.
3. **Improved Readability:** Code that follows SRP is generally more readable because each class or module has a clear and distinct purpose. Developers can quickly understand what each part of the code does.
4. **Reusability:** Classes with single responsibilities are more modular and can be reused in different parts of the application or even in other projects. This promotes code reuse and reduces duplication.
5. **Scalability:** As your application grows and evolves, adhering to SRP makes it easier to extend and adapt the codebase to new requirements. You can add new classes or modify existing ones without affecting unrelated parts of the system.

Practical Application of SRP

To apply SRP effectively, consider the following guidelines:

1. **Identify Responsibilities:** Start by identifying the responsibilities or reasons for change in your application. A responsibility can be defined as a "axis of change," which represents a potential source of modifications.

2. **Separate Responsibilities:** Ensure that each class or module in your codebase has a single, well-defined responsibility. If a class accumulates multiple responsibilities, refactor it into smaller, more focused classes.

3. **Encapsulate Behavior:** Encapsulate behavior related to a specific responsibility within the corresponding class. This encapsulation includes both data and methods.

4. **Maintain a Balance:** While adhering to SRP is essential, avoid creating an excessive number of tiny classes, as this can lead to code that is overly fragmented and harder to maintain. Strive for a balance between granularity and cohesion.

5. **Refactor as Needed:** Continuously review your codebase and refactor when necessary. As your application evolves, new responsibilities may emerge, requiring adjustments to maintain SRP compliance.

In conclusion, the Single Responsibility Principle is a fundamental concept in clean code development that advocates for classes with well-defined responsibilities. By following SRP, you can create code that is easier to maintain, test, and understand, leading to more robust and maintainable software systems.

10.4 Cohesion and Coupling

In the context of clean code and software design, cohesion and coupling are two critical concepts that play a significant role in creating maintainable and efficient code. They are principles that guide the organization and structure of software components, such as classes and modules.

Cohesion

Cohesion refers to the degree to which the responsibilities of a software component (e.g., a class or module) are closely related and focused on a single purpose or functionality. In other words, a cohesive component should have a well-defined and narrowly focused scope. High cohesion is a desirable quality in clean code because it leads to more readable, maintainable, and testable software.

There are several types of cohesion, and they can be ranked from lowest to highest cohesion:

1. **Coincidental Cohesion:** This is the lowest level of cohesion, where the responsibilities of a component are entirely unrelated. Code with coincidental cohesion is challenging to understand and maintain because it lacks a clear purpose.
2. **Logical Cohesion:** In this case, the responsibilities of a component are loosely related by some logical connection, but they don't form a cohesive whole. Code with logical cohesion may still be difficult to understand and modify.
3. **Temporal Cohesion:** Temporal cohesion occurs when the responsibilities of a component are related by the order in which they are executed. While better than coincidental or logical cohesion, this type can still lead to complex and brittle code.
4. **Procedural Cohesion:** In this scenario, the responsibilities are grouped together because they are part of a common procedure or algorithm. This is a step in the right direction,

but it can still be improved.

5. **Communicational Cohesion:** Components with communicational cohesion are responsible for a set of operations that all work on the same data. This is better than procedural cohesion because it groups related operations together.

6. **Sequential Cohesion:** In this case, the responsibilities are related and must be executed in a specific sequence. While it's an improvement, it can often be refactored further.

7. **Functional Cohesion:** This is the highest level of cohesion. A component with functional cohesion has a single, well-defined responsibility or function. It does one thing, and it does it well. Code with functional cohesion is highly maintainable and easy to understand.

Coupling

Coupling refers to the degree to which one software component depends on or is connected to another. Low coupling is desirable in clean code because it promotes modularity and independence between components. Components with low coupling are easier to test, maintain, and reuse.

There are different levels of coupling, ranging from low to high:

1. **No Coupling (or No Dependency):** The ideal scenario where one component doesn't depend on another at all. This is rarely achievable in practice but serves as a reference point for low coupling.

2. **Low Coupling:** Components have limited dependencies on each other, and changes in one component do not significantly impact others. This is a desirable level of coupling.

3. **Moderate Coupling:** Components depend on each other to some extent but are still relatively independent. Changes in one component may require minor adjustments in others.

4. **High Coupling:** Components have strong dependencies on each other, and changes in one component can ripple through the system, requiring extensive modifications in multiple places. High coupling is undesirable and makes the codebase more challenging to maintain.

Balancing Cohesion and Coupling

In clean code development, the goal is to achieve a balance between cohesion and coupling. High cohesion and low coupling are typically the desired states, as they lead to code that is easy to understand, maintain, and extend.

To achieve this balance:

- Strive for functional cohesion within components. Each component should have a clear and well-defined responsibility.

- Reduce dependencies between components. Use interfaces, abstractions, and dependency injection to decouple components when necessary.

- Continuously refactor and review the codebase to identify and address cohesion and coupling issues.

In summary, cohesion and coupling are essential principles in clean code development. Cohesion focuses on the organization of responsibilities within a component, aiming for high functional cohesion. Coupling, on the other hand, deals with the dependencies between components, with the goal of achieving low coupling for increased modularity and maintainability. Balancing these principles contributes to the creation of clean, robust, and maintainable software.

10.5 The Open-Closed Principle (OCP)

The Open-Closed Principle (OCP) is one of the five SOLID principles of object-oriented programming and design. It was formulated by Bertrand Meyer in 1988 and is an essential concept in clean code development. The OCP states that software entities (such as classes, modules, and functions) should be open for extension but closed for modification. In other words, once a software entity is defined and working correctly, it should not be altered to add new functionality or to fix bugs. Instead, the entity should be extended in a way that allows new behavior to be added without changing its existing code.

The primary goal of the Open-Closed Principle is to promote software maintainability, scalability, and robustness. When software entities are open for extension, it becomes easier to adapt and evolve the system over time without introducing unexpected side effects or breaking existing functionality.

Here are some key principles and techniques associated with the Open-Closed Principle:

1. Abstraction and Interfaces

One way to achieve the OCP is by using abstractions, such as interfaces or abstract classes, to define the expected behavior of software entities. Clients of these entities depend on the abstraction rather than the concrete implementation. When new functionality is needed, you can create new implementations of the abstraction without modifying existing code.

For example, consider a geometric shape calculation library with a Shape interface. Adding a new shape (e.g., a triangle) can be done by creating a new class that implements the Shape interface without altering the existing code that works with shapes.

```java
interface Shape {

double area();

}

class Circle implements Shape {

private double radius;

public Circle(double radius) {

this.radius = radius;

}

@Override

public double area() {

return Math.PI * radius * radius;

}

}

class Rectangle implements Shape {

private double width;

private double height;
```

```java
public Rectangle(double width, double height) {

this.width = width;

this.height = height;

}

@Override

public double area() {

return width * height;

}

}
```

// Adding a new shape (e.g., Triangle) can be done by creating a new class implementing the Shape interface.

2. Extension Points

To follow the OCP, you can introduce extension points or hooks in your code that allow for the addition of new functionality. These extension points should be well-defined and designed to minimize the impact on existing code.

For example, a logging framework might provide extension points where developers can plug in custom loggers without modifying the core logging system.

3. Dependency Injection

Dependency Injection (DI) is a technique that promotes the OCP by allowing clients to provide dependencies (e.g., services or implementations) to a component rather than having the component create its own dependencies. This enables you to change the behavior of a component by injecting different dependencies without modifying its code.

4. Use of Design Patterns

Several design patterns, such as the Strategy Pattern and the Decorator Pattern, inherently follow the Open-Closed Principle. These patterns encapsulate behaviors in separate classes or components, making it easy to extend functionality by adding new implementations without altering existing code.

In summary, the Open-Closed Principle is a fundamental concept in clean code development that emphasizes the importance of designing software entities to be open for extension and closed for modification. By using abstractions, extension points, dependency injection, and design patterns, you can create software that is adaptable, maintainable, and scalable over time, minimizing the risk of introducing bugs when adding new features.

Chapter 11: Systems

Section 11.1: The Architecture of Clean Systems

In software development, the architecture of a system is akin to the blueprint of a building. It defines the high-level structure, organization, and components of the software. Clean architecture is an approach that emphasizes separation of concerns, maintainability, and flexibility. In this section, we will delve into the architecture of clean systems and why it's essential for building robust and maintainable software.

The Importance of System Architecture

System architecture plays a pivotal role in software development for several reasons:

1. **Maintainability:** A well-designed architecture makes it easier to maintain and extend the software over time. It ensures that changes to one part of the system do not ripple through the entire codebase.
2. **Scalability:** An architecture that can scale with the growth of the application is crucial. It should accommodate increased loads and changing requirements without significant rework.
3. **Separation of Concerns:** Clean architecture enforces a clear separation of concerns between different parts of the system. This separation makes the codebase more comprehensible and easier to modify.
4. **Testability:** A good architecture facilitates unit testing and automated testing. Isolating components allows for thorough testing, ensuring that the software behaves as expected.

Layers of a Clean System

A clean system architecture often comprises multiple layers, each with its own responsibilities:

1. **Presentation Layer:** This layer is responsible for user interfaces and user interactions. It includes components like web interfaces, mobile app UIs, or command-line interfaces.
2. **Application Layer:** The application layer contains the

business logic of the software. It processes user requests, coordinates data flow, and enforces business rules.

3. **Domain Layer:** At the core of the system is the domain layer, which encapsulates the business logic and entities specific to the application domain. It should be independent of external frameworks and technologies.

4. **Infrastructure Layer:** The infrastructure layer deals with external concerns such as databases, external services, and communication protocols. It provides the necessary interfaces for the application layer to interact with external resources.

Dependency Inversion Principle (DIP)

One of the fundamental principles in clean system architecture is the Dependency Inversion Principle (DIP). It suggests that high-level modules should not depend on low-level modules but both should depend on abstractions. In other words, the direction of dependency should be inverted.

By adhering to DIP, you ensure that your system is loosely coupled, making it more adaptable to changes. It also allows for the easy replacement of components, as long as they adhere to the same abstractions.

In summary, clean system architecture is a cornerstone of building maintainable and scalable software. It involves organizing the codebase into distinct layers, adhering to the Dependency Inversion Principle, and emphasizing separation of concerns. In the following sections, we will explore these concepts in more detail and provide practical guidance on designing clean systems.

Section 11.2: Separating High-Level Policy

from Low-Level Details

Clean system architecture encourages the separation of high-level policy from low-level details. This principle, often referred to as the separation of concerns, is instrumental in designing systems that are maintainable, adaptable, and testable. In this section, we will explore the concept in depth and understand why it is crucial in clean code practices.

Understanding Separation of Concerns

Separation of concerns is a design principle that advocates dividing a system into distinct sections, where each section addresses a specific aspect or concern of the software. These concerns can vary widely, from business rules and user interfaces to data storage and infrastructure.

The primary goals of separation of concerns are as follows:

1. **Maintainability:** By isolating each concern, it becomes easier to modify or extend one aspect of the system without affecting others. This reduces the risk of introducing unintended side effects.
2. **Readability:** Separation of concerns makes the codebase more comprehensible. Developers can focus on a specific aspect of the system without being overwhelmed by unrelated details.
3. **Testability:** When concerns are separated, it becomes simpler to write unit tests for individual components. This enables more effective testing of the system's functionality.

High-Level Policy

High-level policy refers to the core business rules, logic, and decisions that drive the behavior of the software. These policies are typically unique to the application domain and should be isolated from implementation details and external dependencies.

In clean system architecture, high-level policies are usually found in the domain layer. This layer contains the business entities, rules, and use cases that define the application's behavior. By keeping high-level policies separate from low-level details, you create a clear and stable foundation for your system.

Low-Level Details

Low-level details, on the other hand, encompass implementation specifics, external interactions, and technical intricacies. This includes database access, network communication, user interface rendering, and more. These details are essential for the system to function but should be decoupled from the high-level policies.

In clean architecture, low-level details are typically relegated to the infrastructure layer. This layer provides the necessary interfaces to interact with external systems and resources. By isolating these details, you ensure that changes to infrastructure components do not disrupt the core business logic.

Benefits of Separation

The benefits of separating high-level policy from low-level details are significant:

- **Flexibility:** You can modify low-level details or swap out components without affecting the high-level policy. This flexibility is crucial for adapting to evolving requirements and technologies.

- **Testability:** High-level policies are easier to unit test when they are isolated from external dependencies. This allows for thorough testing of the core functionality.

- **Clarity:** Code that follows the separation of concerns principle tends to be more readable and understandable. Developers can grasp the intent of each component more easily.

Practical Implementation

To implement the separation of concerns, consider using design patterns like the Dependency Injection pattern. Dependency injection allows you to inject high-level policies into low-level components without them being tightly coupled. Additionally, defining clear interfaces and adhering to the SOLID principles can aid in achieving this separation.

In the next sections, we will delve deeper into these concepts and explore practical examples of clean system architecture. Separating high-level policy from low-level details is a key step in building systems that are both maintainable and adaptable to change.

Section 11.3: Dependency Inversion Principle (DIP)

The Dependency Inversion Principle (DIP) is one of the five SOLID principles of object-oriented design, and it plays a crucial role in clean system architecture. DIP is often considered the "D" in SOLID, and its primary objective is to establish a clear and flexible relationship between high-level policy and low-level details, enabling clean code practices.

Understanding the Dependency Inversion Principle

DIP can be summarized as follows: "High-level modules should not depend on low-level modules. Both should depend on abstractions." This principle encourages the following concepts:

1. **Abstraction:** In the context of DIP, abstraction refers to defining interfaces or abstract classes that represent the high-level policies and low-level details of a system. These abstractions act as contracts that specify what behavior is expected.
2. **Decoupling:** By depending on abstractions rather than concrete implementations, high-level and low-level modules become independent of each other. This decoupling is essential for maintaining clean code because it reduces dependencies and minimizes the impact of changes.

Dependency Inversion in Practice

To apply the Dependency Inversion Principle effectively, consider the following practices:

1. Define Abstractions:

Start by defining clear abstractions that represent the high-level policies and low-level details in your system. These abstractions should be defined as interfaces or abstract classes.

2. *Implement Abstractions:*

Implement concrete classes that adhere to these abstractions. These implementations represent the specific high-level policies and low-level details of your application.

3. *Inversion of Control (IoC):*

Implement Inversion of Control (IoC) containers or frameworks to manage the instantiation and wiring of dependencies. IoC containers facilitate the injection of concrete implementations into high-level modules, adhering to the DIP.

4. *Dependency Injection (DI):*

Use Dependency Injection to inject the required dependencies (abstractions) into high-level modules. This injection ensures that high-level modules do not depend on concrete implementations but rather on abstractions.

5. *Favor Composition:*

Prefer composition over inheritance to achieve DIP. This means that you should compose your objects by injecting dependencies rather than relying on inheritance hierarchies.

6. *Abstraction Layers:*

Organize your codebase into layers that reflect different levels of abstraction. For example, you might have a domain layer with high-level policies and an infrastructure layer with low-level details. Abstractions should span these layers.

Benefits of the Dependency Inversion Principle

Applying DIP brings several advantages to clean code and system architecture:

- **Reduced Coupling:** High-level and low-level modules become loosely coupled, making it easier to modify, replace, or extend components without affecting others.

- **Testability:** Abstractions allow for the use of mock objects and stubs in testing, enabling thorough and isolated unit testing.

- **Adaptability:** DIP promotes flexibility by allowing you to change implementations while adhering to the same abstractions.

- **Understanding:** Code that follows DIP principles is often more readable and understandable since it separates concerns and clarifies dependencies.

In summary, the Dependency Inversion Principle is a fundamental concept in clean code and system architecture. By adhering to DIP and using abstractions to separate high-level policy from low-level details, you can create more maintainable, flexible, and testable code. In the following sections, we will explore additional clean code principles and practices that further enhance software quality.

Section 11.4: High-Level Modules and Abstraction

In the context of clean code and software architecture, high-level modules play a crucial role in defining the overall structure and behavior of a system. These modules are responsible for orchestrating and coordinating various components and low-level modules to fulfill the system's higher-level goals. To achieve clean code and maintainable systems, it's essential to understand the significance of high-level modules and the role of abstraction within them.

The Role of High-Level Modules

High-level modules, sometimes referred to as "top-level modules" or "policy modules," represent the core functionality and business logic of a software system. They encapsulate the system's high-level policies and domain-specific rules. Here are some key characteristics and responsibilities of high-level modules:

1. **Abstraction of Complexity:** High-level modules abstract away the intricacies and complexities of lower-level details. They provide a simplified and coherent interface to the rest of the system.

2. **Decision Making:** These modules are responsible for making decisions based on business rules, user input, or external factors. They define the system's behavior in response to various scenarios.

3. **Coordination:** High-level modules coordinate the activities of lower-level modules and components. They decide when and how lower-level operations should be executed to achieve the desired results.

4. **Loose Coupling:** Clean code promotes loose coupling between high-level and low-level modules. High-level modules should depend on abstractions (as per the Dependency Inversion Principle) rather than concrete implementations.

5. **Testability:** Separating high-level policies into distinct modules enhances testability. You can write focused tests for high-level functionality without being concerned about

the details of lower-level components.

Abstraction Within High-Level Modules

Abstraction is a key concept within high-level modules. It involves the use of abstract classes, interfaces, or well-defined contracts to represent the behavior and expectations of a module. Here's how abstraction contributes to clean code within high-level modules:

1. **Clear Contracts:** Abstraction defines clear contracts that specify what a high-level module expects from lower-level components. This contract helps developers understand the responsibilities and interactions of each module.
2. **Flexibility:** Abstraction allows for flexibility in implementation. High-level modules can work with different concrete implementations as long as they adhere to the defined abstraction.
3. **Maintenance:** When changes are required, such as replacing a component or adding a new feature, the abstraction acts as a safeguard. It ensures that changes in lower-level components do not disrupt the functioning of high-level modules.
4. **Testing:** Abstractions facilitate unit testing by allowing for the use of mock objects or stubs to isolate high-level modules during testing.

Example of Abstraction in High-Level Modules

Consider a high-level module responsible for processing online orders in an e-commerce application. This module defines an abstraction called OrderProcessor:

public interface OrderProcessor {

```
void processOrder(Order order);

}
```

The OrderProcessor interface abstracts the process of order handling without specifying how orders should be processed. Multiple concrete implementations can exist, each handling orders differently (e.g., processing payments, updating inventory, sending confirmation emails).

By adhering to this abstraction, the high-level module can work with different OrderProcessor implementations, making the system more adaptable and maintainable.

In conclusion, high-level modules and abstraction are essential components of clean code and robust software architecture. They enable the separation of concerns, maintainability, and flexibility in software systems. By properly defining abstractions and adhering to them within high-level modules, developers can achieve clean, modular, and maintainable codebases.

Section 11.5: The Main Program and the Structure of Systems

The main program of a software system serves as its entry point and orchestrates the execution of various components, modules, and functionalities. In clean code and software architecture, designing the main program and structuring the system effectively is crucial for readability, maintainability, and scalability. This section explores the role of the main program and the principles for organizing system structure.

The Role of the Main Program

1. **Initialization:** The main program is responsible for initializing the core components and services needed for the system to operate. This includes setting up data sources, configuring services, and preparing the environment.
2. **Control Flow:** It defines the high-level control flow of the application. This involves determining the order in which various operations and components are executed.
3. **Error Handling:** The main program often handles global error and exception handling. It defines how the system should react to unexpected issues and exceptions, ensuring graceful degradation when errors occur.
4. **Resource Management:** It oversees the management of critical resources, such as database connections, file handles, and network sockets. Proper resource management helps prevent resource leaks and performance issues.

Principles for Structuring Systems

1. **Modularity:** Break down the system into smaller, manageable modules or components. Each module should have a well-defined responsibility and interface. This promotes reusability and ease of testing.
2. **Separation of Concerns:** Follow the principle of separating different concerns within the system. For example, separate user interface logic from business logic and data access logic. This separation simplifies maintenance and promotes clean code.
3. **Dependency Management:** Use dependency injection or inversion of control (IoC) to manage dependencies between components. This reduces coupling and makes it

easier to replace or upgrade individual parts of the system.

4. **Layered Architecture:** Consider organizing the system into layers, such as presentation, business logic, and data access layers. Each layer has a specific responsibility, and interactions between layers should follow clear boundaries and contracts.

5. **Use Design Patterns:** Leverage design patterns like the Model-View-Controller (MVC), Dependency Injection, and Observer patterns to solve common architectural problems. These patterns provide well-established solutions to recurring challenges.

Example of System Structure

Let's consider an example of structuring a web application:

- **Presentation Layer:** This layer handles user interface and user interactions. It includes components like controllers, views, and templates. In a clean code approach, controllers should focus on handling user input and delegating business logic to the next layer.

- **Business Logic Layer:** Also known as the service layer, this component contains the core business logic of the application. It communicates with the presentation layer to receive user requests, processes them, and interacts with the data access layer to retrieve or store data.

- **Data Access Layer:** Responsible for interacting with data storage, such as databases or external services. It encapsulates data retrieval and storage operations and provides a clean interface for the business logic layer to access data.

- **Main Program:** The main program serves as the entry point to the application. It initializes the necessary components, sets up routing, handles errors, and defines the overall control flow of the application.

Here's a simplified example in Python:

```python
# Main Program

if __name__ == "__main__":
    # Initialize components
    data_source = initialize_data_source()

    service_layer = initialize_service_layer(data_source)

    presentation_layer = initialize_presentation_layer(service_layer)

    # Start the application

    presentation_layer.run()
```

In this example, the main program initializes the components, starting from the data source to the presentation layer. It orchestrates the application's execution, adhering to the principles of clean code and system structure.

In conclusion, designing the main program and structuring a software system are critical aspects of clean code and software architecture. By following modularity, separation of concerns, proper dependency management, and other architectural principles, developers can create systems that are more maintainable, scalable, and easier to understand.

Chapter 12: Emergence

Section 12.1: What Is Emergent Design?

Emergent design is a software development approach that emphasizes the evolution of design over time based on the changing needs and requirements of a project. It contrasts with the traditional "Big Design Up Front" (BDUF) approach, where all design decisions are made before any code is written. Emergent design embraces the idea that the best design often emerges gradually as developers gain a deeper understanding of the problem domain and as the software evolves.

Key Principles of Emergent Design:

1. **Simplicity:** Emergent design encourages simplicity in software. Rather than trying to anticipate all possible future requirements upfront, developers focus on the current needs and aim to create a simple and working solution.
2. **Feedback Loop:** It relies on a continuous feedback loop. Developers write code, test it, and gather feedback. This feedback informs subsequent design decisions, allowing the design to adapt and improve over time.
3. **Evolutionary:** Design evolves as the project progresses. Developers refactor and improve code as they learn more about the problem domain and discover better ways to implement functionality.
4. **Incremental:** Emergent design is incremental. Developers start with a basic structure and incrementally add features and improvements. This approach reduces the risk of over-engineering.

Benefits of Emergent Design:

- **Flexibility:** Emergent design allows for flexibility in responding to changing requirements. Developers can adapt the software to meet new needs without being constrained by a rigid initial design.

- **Reduced Waste:** It minimizes the waste of resources on unnecessary design work that may not be used. Developers focus their efforts on areas that provide the most value.

- **Better Understanding:** Developers gain a better understanding of the problem domain and the system's behavior through hands-on coding and feedback.

- **Higher Quality:** By continuously improving the design, emergent design often results in higher-quality software that is easier to maintain and extend.

When to Use Emergent Design:

Emergent design is particularly well-suited for:

- **Complex Projects:** Projects with uncertain or evolving requirements benefit from the adaptability of emergent design.

- **Research and Development:** In research-oriented projects, where the final solution is not entirely clear from the outset, emergent design allows for experimentation and discovery.

- **Startups and Prototyping:** Startups and prototypes often require quick development to validate ideas. Emergent design enables rapid iterations.

Emergent Design in Practice:

In practice, emergent design aligns with agile development methodologies, such as Scrum or Extreme Programming (XP). These methodologies promote iterative development, frequent releases, and collaboration with stakeholders.

Developers practicing emergent design focus on writing clean, maintainable code. They refactor as needed to improve the design, and they use automated tests to ensure that changes do not introduce regressions.

While emergent design is valuable, it's essential to strike a balance. Some level of upfront design and architecture may still be necessary, especially for projects with critical performance or security requirements. The key is to avoid over-engineering and to adapt the design as the project progresses and requirements become clearer.

Section 12.2: Patterns and Design Smells

In the realm of software development, patterns and design smells are two concepts that play a significant role in emergent design. They help developers make informed design decisions and identify areas of improvement within their codebase.

Design Patterns:

Design patterns are well-established solutions to recurring problems in software design. They provide templates for solving common architectural and structural issues, making it easier to create robust and maintainable code. Some of the most well-known design patterns include the Singleton, Factory, Observer, and Strategy patterns.

Benefits of Design Patterns:

- **Reuse:** Design patterns promote code reuse. Instead of reinventing the wheel, developers can apply proven solutions to similar problems.

- **Scalability:** Patterns help create flexible and scalable architectures that can adapt to changing requirements.

- **Maintainability:** Code built around design patterns tends to be more maintainable and easier to understand since it follows recognized conventions.

- **Communication:** Design patterns provide a common vocabulary for developers to discuss and document architectural decisions.

- **Quality:** Applying design patterns often leads to higher-quality code with reduced bugs and easier testing.

However, it's crucial to apply design patterns judiciously. Overusing patterns can lead to overly complex code, which is contrary to the principles of emergent design. Developers should aim to strike a balance by identifying where patterns are genuinely beneficial.

Design Smells:

Design smells are indicators of potential issues or areas for improvement in the code. They are not necessarily bugs, but they suggest that there might be a problem with the design. Recognizing and addressing design smells is an essential part of emergent design.

Common Design Smells:

1. **God Class:** A class that does too much and has too many responsibilities.
2. **Duplicated Code:** Repeated code segments throughout the codebase.
3. **Large Method:** Methods that are overly long and complex.
4. **Inappropriate Intimacy:** Classes that are too tightly coupled, violating the principle of loose coupling.
5. **Feature Envy:** A class that is overly interested in the internal state of another class.
6. **Refused Bequest:** Subclasses that inherit from a superclass but don't use all the inherited features.
7. **Data Class:** A class with little or no behavior, primarily serving as a data container.

Addressing Design Smells:

Identifying design smells is the first step to addressing them. Tools like static code analyzers and code reviews can help spot design smells in the codebase. Once identified, developers can refactor the code to eliminate or reduce the smells.

The goal of addressing design smells is to improve code quality, maintainability, and readability. It aligns with the principles of emergent design by continuously refining the codebase as the project evolves.

In conclusion, design patterns and design smells are valuable tools for developers practicing emergent design. Design patterns offer reusable solutions to common problems, while design smells highlight areas in need of improvement. By applying both concepts effectively, developers can create software that adapts to changing requirements, is easier to maintain, and meets high-quality standards.

Section 12.3: Refactoring and Clean Code

Refactoring is a fundamental practice in software development that aligns closely with the principles of clean code and emergent design. It involves making incremental changes to the codebase to improve its structure, readability, and maintainability without altering its external behavior. The goal of refactoring is to keep the codebase in good health throughout its lifecycle.

The Role of Refactoring:

Refactoring plays a pivotal role in maintaining and enhancing software systems:

1. **Maintainability:** Over time, code can become messy and hard to understand. Refactoring helps keep the codebase clean and easy to maintain, reducing the cost of future development.
2. **Readability:** Clean code is more readable, making it easier for developers to understand and work with. This leads to fewer errors and faster development.
3. **Bug Reduction:** Refactoring can uncover and eliminate hidden bugs and issues in the code. It often reveals problems that might not be apparent through casual code review.
4. **Scalability:** Well-refactored code is more scalable and adaptable to changing requirements. It can accommodate

new features and enhancements with minimal disruption.

5. **Collaboration:** Clean code encourages collaboration among team members. When code is easy to understand, team members can work together more effectively.

Refactoring Techniques:

Refactoring encompasses various techniques, each aimed at improving specific aspects of the code:

1. **Extract Method:** This technique involves breaking down a large method into smaller, more manageable ones. It improves code readability and makes it easier to reuse code fragments.

2. **Rename:** Giving meaningful names to variables, functions, and classes is essential for clean code. Renaming improves code clarity and helps developers understand the purpose of each element.

3. **Remove Duplication:** Eliminating duplicated code improves maintainability and reduces the chances of introducing errors when making changes.

4. **Simplify Conditionals:** Complex conditional statements can be simplified to make code more readable and less error-prone.

5. **Encapsulate:** Encapsulation involves grouping related data and functions into classes or modules. It enhances code organization and reduces coupling between components.

6. **Replace Magic Numbers with Constants:** Replacing magic numbers with named constants makes code more self-explanatory and easier to modify.

The Refactoring Workflow:

Refactoring should be performed systematically and safely. Here's a typical workflow for refactoring:

1. **Identify Areas for Improvement:** Use code reviews, static analysis tools, and personal experience to identify areas of the code that need refactoring.
2. **Write Tests:** Before refactoring, write tests to ensure that the existing code behaves correctly. These tests serve as a safety net.
3. **Make Small, Incremental Changes:** Refactor one small piece of code at a time, ensuring that each step maintains the code's correctness.
4. **Run Tests:** After each refactoring step, run the tests to verify that the code still behaves as expected. If a test fails, fix it immediately.
5. **Review and Document:** Document the changes made during refactoring and ensure that the code remains clean and readable.
6. **Repeat:** Continue this cycle until the desired improvements are achieved.

Emergent Design and Refactoring:

Refactoring is an integral part of emergent design. As the software evolves, design decisions may need to be adjusted. Refactoring allows the codebase to adapt to changing requirements while maintaining its quality. By continuously refining the design through refactoring, developers can create code that is both clean and flexible.

In conclusion, refactoring is a key practice that complements clean code and emergent design principles. It helps maintain code quality, readability, and adaptability throughout the software's lifecycle. By embracing refactoring techniques and workflows, development teams can create and sustain software systems that are robust, maintainable, and aligned with evolving requirements.

Section 12.4: Pragmatic vs. Dogmatic Design

In the world of software development, two contrasting design philosophies often emerge: pragmatic design and dogmatic design. Both approaches have their merits and are valuable in different contexts. This section explores these two design philosophies and discusses when each one is most appropriate.

Pragmatic Design:

Pragmatic design, as the name suggests, is grounded in practicality and flexibility. It prioritizes the immediate needs of a project and aims for simplicity and quick results. Key characteristics of pragmatic design include:

1. **Focus on Delivering Value:** Pragmatic design is result-oriented. It aims to deliver value to users or stakeholders as quickly as possible, even if it means taking shortcuts or making trade-offs.
2. **Iterative and Adaptive:** Pragmatic designers are open to change and iteration. They believe that it's okay to refactor or redesign when necessary to accommodate evolving requirements.
3. **Real-World Constraints:** Pragmatic designers understand that real-world projects often have constraints, such as time and budget limitations. They work within these constraints to achieve the best possible outcomes.
4. **Balanced Perfection:** Rather than striving for perfection, pragmatic design seeks a balance between quality and

speed. It's willing to accept a certain level of technical debt to meet immediate goals.

5. **Focus on User Needs:** Pragmatic designers prioritize meeting the needs of users and stakeholders. They are willing to make design decisions that may not align with theoretical best practices if it serves the users' needs better.

Dogmatic Design:

Dogmatic design, on the other hand, adheres strictly to established principles and best practices, often without compromise. It aims for a "perfect" design based on theoretical ideals. Key characteristics of dogmatic design include:

1. **Adherence to Principles:** Dogmatic designers strictly adhere to established design principles and guidelines, such as SOLID principles or design patterns.

2. **Long-Term Vision:** Dogmatic design often focuses on the long-term maintainability and scalability of a system. It's willing to invest more time and effort upfront to create a robust foundation.

3. **Resistance to Change:** Dogmatic designers may be resistant to changing their initial design decisions, even when new requirements emerge. They prioritize sticking to the original plan.

4. **Minimization of Technical Debt:** Dogmatic designers strive to minimize technical debt from the outset, believing that it can lead to a more maintainable codebase in the long run.

5. **Emphasis on Best Practices:** Dogmatic design emphasizes best practices and theoretical ideals over practicality. It seeks to create an "ideal" design, even if it takes longer to achieve.

Choosing the Right Approach:

The choice between pragmatic and dogmatic design depends on several factors, including the nature of the project, the team's experience, and the project's goals. Here are some considerations:

- **Project Stage:** Pragmatic design may be more suitable for rapid prototyping or early development stages when requirements are evolving. Dogmatic design may be better for mature projects with stable requirements.

- **Team Expertise:** The experience and expertise of the development team play a role. Highly skilled teams may find dogmatic design more feasible, while less experienced teams may benefit from the flexibility of pragmatic design.

- **Resource Constraints:** Consider time and budget constraints. Projects with tight deadlines or limited resources may need to lean toward pragmatic design to meet immediate goals.

- **User-Centricity:** If the project's success depends heavily on meeting specific user needs, pragmatic design may be the better choice, as it prioritizes delivering value quickly.

In practice, a blend of both approaches is often the most effective. Pragmatic design can help a project get off the ground and adapt to changing circumstances, while dogmatic design can provide a solid foundation for long-term maintainability. The key is to strike the right balance based on the project's unique context and constraints.

Section 12.5: Designing with Simplicity and Flexibility

In the quest for clean code and effective software design, simplicity and flexibility stand out as two vital principles. While they may seem contradictory at first glance, they can coexist harmoniously in well-crafted software systems. This section delves into the importance of designing with simplicity and flexibility in mind and how to strike the right balance between them.

The Value of Simplicity:

Simplicity in software design is akin to Occam's razor, which suggests that the simplest explanation or solution is often the best. Simplicity contributes to clean code by reducing complexity and making it easier to understand, maintain, and extend. Here are some key aspects of designing with simplicity:

1. **Readability:** Simple code is more readable. It uses clear and concise constructs, making it easier for developers to grasp the logic and intent.
2. **Maintenance:** Simple code is less error-prone and easier to maintain. When bugs or changes are needed, developers can navigate and modify the codebase with confidence.
3. **Scalability:** Simplicity fosters scalability. It's easier to build upon a simple foundation and extend functionality without introducing unnecessary complications.
4. **Debugging:** Simple code simplifies the debugging process. When issues arise, it's easier to identify the root cause in straightforward code.
5. **Reducing Technical Debt:** Simplicity helps in minimizing technical debt, as it avoids unnecessary complexity that may accumulate over time.

The Need for Flexibility:

While simplicity is essential, software systems must also be flexible to adapt to changing requirements and environments. Here's why flexibility matters:

1. **Adaptability:** Flexible code can adapt to new features, technologies, and requirements without requiring significant rework.
2. **Future-Proofing:** Building with flexibility in mind future-proofs your software. It can accommodate changes that were unforeseen during the initial design phase.
3. **Customization:** Flexible code can be tailored to specific use cases or customized for different clients or users.
4. **Integration:** In a world of diverse technologies, flexible code can integrate with various systems, APIs, and data sources.
5. **User Feedback:** Flexibility allows you to incorporate user feedback and pivot when necessary.

Balancing Simplicity and Flexibility:

Achieving the right balance between simplicity and flexibility can be challenging but is crucial for sustainable software design. Here are some strategies:

1. **KISS Principle:** Follow the "Keep It Simple, Stupid" principle. Start with the simplest design that meets the current requirements.
2. **YAGNI Principle:** Embrace the "You Ain't Gonna Need It" principle. Don't over-engineer by adding unnecessary features or complexity prematurely.
3. **Separation of Concerns:** Use design patterns and principles like the Single Responsibility Principle (SRP) to

separate concerns and promote simplicity.

4. **Refactoring:** Regularly review and refactor code to maintain simplicity while adding flexibility where needed.
5. **Modular Design:** Break down systems into modular components that can be extended or replaced individually.
6. **Testing:** Comprehensive testing, including unit tests and integration tests, helps ensure that flexibility doesn't compromise correctness.
7. **Documentation:** Clear and concise documentation can aid in understanding and maintaining both simple and flexible code.
8. **User-Centricity:** Prioritize user needs and feedback. Simplicity and flexibility should serve the user's goals.

In conclusion, designing with simplicity and flexibility requires a thoughtful and balanced approach. Simplicity enhances code readability and maintainability, while flexibility ensures that the code can adapt to evolving requirements. Both principles should serve the ultimate goal of delivering clean, reliable, and user-centric software.

Chapter 13: Concurrency

Section 13.1: Understanding Concurrency Challenges

Concurrency is a fundamental aspect of modern software development, especially in applications that need to handle multiple tasks simultaneously. It allows software to make efficient use of multi-core processors and improves responsiveness. However, it introduces complex challenges that developers must understand and manage.

What Is Concurrency?

Concurrency refers to the ability of a system to perform multiple tasks simultaneously. These tasks can be threads, processes, or even independent units of work within a single thread. Concurrency enables applications to be more responsive and utilize available hardware resources efficiently.

Challenges in Concurrent Programming:

While concurrency offers many benefits, it also brings several challenges:

1. **Race Conditions:** Race conditions occur when multiple threads or processes access shared data concurrently, leading to unexpected behavior or data corruption. To mitigate race conditions, synchronization mechanisms like locks and semaphores are used.
2. **Deadlocks:** Deadlocks happen when multiple threads or processes are waiting for resources held by others, causing all of them to halt indefinitely. Detecting and resolving

deadlocks require careful design and monitoring.

3. **Data Corruption:** Concurrent access to shared data can result in data corruption if not properly managed. Techniques like atomic operations and memory barriers help maintain data integrity.

4. **Performance Bottlenecks:** Poorly designed concurrent systems can suffer from performance bottlenecks, defeating the purpose of concurrency. Profiling and performance tuning are essential to identify and eliminate bottlenecks.

5. **Complex Debugging:** Debugging concurrent code is notoriously difficult due to non-deterministic behavior. Reproducing and diagnosing issues can be time-consuming.

Concurrency Models:

Several concurrency models and paradigms exist to address these challenges:

1. **Multithreading:** In multithreading, multiple threads run within a single process, sharing memory space. While it offers efficient communication and resource sharing, it also requires careful synchronization to avoid issues.

2. **Multiprocessing:** Multiprocessing involves running multiple independent processes, each with its memory space. This approach provides isolation but requires inter-process communication mechanisms.

3. **Message Passing:** Message passing models, like the actor model, emphasize communication between isolated entities (actors or processes) through message passing. This can simplify concurrency by avoiding shared memory concerns.

Tools and Libraries:

To address concurrency challenges, various tools and libraries are available in different programming languages. Some popular ones include:

- **Java Concurrency API:** Provides tools like threads, thread pools, and synchronization primitives.

- **Python's asyncio:** Allows asynchronous programming with coroutines for I/O-bound tasks.

- **C++ Standard Library:** Offers thread management and synchronization primitives.

- **Go's Goroutines:** Lightweight threads that simplify concurrent programming.

When to Use Concurrency:

Concurrency is not a one-size-fits-all solution. It's essential to evaluate whether your application truly benefits from concurrency. Use concurrency when:

- Your application performs I/O-bound or CPU-bound tasks that can be parallelized.

- You need to improve responsiveness, such as in GUI applications.

- You have a multi-core processor or distributed system.

In conclusion, concurrency is a powerful tool that, when used judiciously, can enhance the performance and responsiveness of software applications. However, it comes with challenges that require careful consideration and proper handling. Understanding the principles and tools of concurrency is essential for building robust and efficient concurrent systems.

Section 13.2: Writing Safe Concurrent Code

Writing safe concurrent code is a challenging task that requires careful consideration of race conditions, data sharing, and synchronization. In this section, we'll explore best practices and techniques for ensuring the safety and correctness of concurrent programs.

Immutable Data Structures

One of the most effective ways to mitigate concurrency issues is to use immutable data structures. Immutable objects cannot be modified once created, eliminating the need for locks and synchronization. Instead, when you need to modify an immutable object, you create a new one with the desired changes. This approach ensures thread safety by design.

```java
// Example of an immutable class in Java

public final class ImmutablePoint {

private final int x;

private final int y;

public ImmutablePoint(int x, int y) {

this.x = x;

this.y = y;

}
```

```
public int getX() {

return x;

}

public int getY() {

return y;

}

}
```

Thread-Local Storage

Thread-local storage (TLS) allows each thread to have its own private data that other threads cannot access. This can be useful when you have data that is specific to a particular thread's execution. Most programming languages provide mechanisms for implementing TLS.

In Java, you can use ThreadLocal:

```
private static ThreadLocal<DateFormat> dateFormatThreadLocal
=         ThreadLocal.withInitial(()        ->        new
SimpleDateFormat("yyyy-MM-dd"));
```

Lock-Free and Non-Blocking Algorithms

Lock-free and non-blocking algorithms aim to provide thread safety without traditional locks. These algorithms are complex but can be highly efficient in situations where contention for locks would be a bottleneck.

For example, Java's java.util.concurrent package includes non-blocking data structures like ConcurrentHashMap and CopyOnWriteArrayList.

Proper Use of Locks

When locks are necessary, they should be used judiciously. Avoid holding locks for extended periods to prevent contention and performance degradation. Use fine-grained locks whenever possible to minimize contention.

```java
// Using fine-grained locks in Java

private final Object lock1 = new Object();

private final Object lock2 = new Object();

public void performComplexTask() {

synchronized (lock1) {

// Critical section 1

}

synchronized (lock2) {

// Critical section 2

}

}
```

Testing and Debugging

Testing concurrent code is challenging due to its non-deterministic nature. It's essential to create comprehensive unit tests that cover various scenarios, including edge cases and contention situations.

Tools like thread analyzers and profilers can help identify and debug concurrency issues.

Avoiding Shared Mutable State

A fundamental principle in writing concurrent code is to avoid shared mutable state whenever possible. Shared mutable state is a breeding ground for race conditions and data corruption. Instead, consider using message passing, actor models, or other paradigms that promote isolation and immutability.

Conclusion

Concurrency is a powerful tool for improving the performance of software systems, but it comes with inherent challenges. Writing safe concurrent code requires a deep understanding of concurrency concepts, careful design, and rigorous testing. By following best practices such as using immutable data structures, thread-local storage, and proper synchronization, developers can create concurrent programs that are both efficient and correct.

Section 13.3: Encapsulating Shared State

Encapsulating shared state is a critical aspect of writing concurrent code that is both safe and maintainable. In this section, we'll explore the importance of encapsulation and various techniques for managing shared state in concurrent programs.

The Challenge of Shared State

Shared state refers to data that multiple threads can access and potentially modify concurrently. When not handled properly, shared state can lead to race conditions, data corruption, and bugs that are hard to reproduce and debug. Therefore, it's essential to encapsulate shared state to limit direct access and modification by multiple threads.

Encapsulation through Object-Oriented Principles

Encapsulation, one of the core principles of object-oriented programming, involves bundling data and methods that operate on that data into a single unit known as a class. In concurrent programming, classes can serve as encapsulated containers for shared state, allowing you to control access and modification.

Here's an example in Java:

```java
public class SharedCounter {

private int count;

public SharedCounter() {

count = 0;

}

public synchronized void increment() {

count++;

}

public synchronized int getCount() {

return count;

}

}
```

In this example, the SharedCounter class encapsulates the shared state (the count variable) and provides synchronized methods for safe access and modification.

Using Locks and Synchronization

Locks and synchronization mechanisms, such as the synchronized keyword in Java, help ensure that only one thread can access a critical section of code at a time. By applying locks to shared state access, you can prevent concurrent modification and enforce thread safety.

```java
public class SharedResource {

private final Object lock = new Object();

private int data;

public void updateData(int newValue) {

synchronized (lock) {

data = newValue;

}

}

public int readData() {

synchronized (lock) {

return data;

}

}

}
```

In this example, the synchronized blocks protect the data field, ensuring that only one thread can update or read it at a time.

Immutable Data Structures

As mentioned in the previous section, using immutable data structures is an effective way to encapsulate shared state. Immutable objects cannot be modified once created, eliminating the need for locks and synchronization. When you need to modify the data, you create a new immutable object with the desired changes.

Message Passing

Message passing is an alternative approach to managing shared state by isolating it within individual threads or actors. Threads communicate by sending messages to each other rather than directly accessing shared data. This paradigm promotes encapsulation and reduces the risk of race conditions.

Conclusion

Encapsulating shared state is a fundamental practice in concurrent programming. By using object-oriented principles, locks, synchronization, immutable data structures, or message passing, you can control access to shared data and reduce the risk of concurrency-related issues. Effective encapsulation not only ensures thread safety but also improves code maintainability and comprehensibility in complex concurrent systems.

Section 13.4: Choosing the Right Concurrency Tools

In concurrent programming, choosing the right concurrency tools and libraries is crucial to building robust and efficient multi-threaded applications. The choice of tools depends on the programming language, the specific requirements of your application, and your familiarity with different concurrency models. This section explores various concurrency tools and considerations for their selection.

Threads and Thread Pools

One of the most basic forms of concurrency is using threads. Threads allow you to run multiple tasks concurrently within a single process. However, managing threads manually can be error-prone and may lead to issues like resource leaks or thread contention. Thread pools are a higher-level abstraction that manages a pool of worker threads, making it easier to control thread creation and lifecycle.

In Java, you can use the ExecutorService and related classes to work with thread pools:

ExecutorService executor = Executors.newFixedThreadPool(4); // *Create a thread pool with 4 threads*

executor.submit(() -> { /* *Your task code here* */ });

Fork-Join Framework

The fork-join framework, introduced in Java, is designed for parallelism in divide-and-conquer algorithms. It's particularly useful when breaking down a large task into smaller subtasks that can be processed concurrently and then merged together.

ForkJoinPool pool = **new** ForkJoinPool();

Result result = pool.invoke(**new** MyRecursiveTask()); // *MyRecursiveTask is your task implementation*

Asynchronous Programming

Asynchronous programming models, often seen in languages like JavaScript and Python, allow you to perform non-blocking I/O operations and handle concurrency with event-driven callbacks or async/await syntax. These models are well-suited for I/O-bound tasks and event-driven applications.

```javascript
// Node.js example

const fs = require('fs');

fs.readFile('file.txt', 'utf8', (err, data) => {

if (err) throw err;

console.log(data);

});
```

Actor Model

The actor model is a concurrency model that abstracts concurrency through actors, which are independent entities that communicate by sending messages. Languages like Erlang and Elixir are known for their strong support of the actor model, making them suitable for building highly concurrent and fault-tolerant systems.

```elixir
# Elixir example

defmodule MyActor do

def act do

receive do

{:message, content} -> IO.puts("Received: #{content}")
```

end

end

end

Concurrency Libraries

Many programming languages offer concurrency libraries and frameworks that simplify concurrent programming. For example, Python provides the concurrent.futures module for high-level concurrent and parallel programming. C++ offers the C++ Standard Library's <thread> and <future> headers for threading and futures.

Considerations for Choosing Concurrency Tools

When choosing concurrency tools, consider the following factors:

1. **Application Requirements**: Identify whether your application is compute-bound or I/O-bound, as this affects the choice of concurrency model and tools.
2. **Language Support**: Different languages offer varying levels of support for concurrency. Choose tools that align with your programming language.
3. **Ease of Use**: Some tools are more straightforward to use than others. Consider your team's expertise and the learning curve associated with the tools.
4. **Scalability**: Ensure that the chosen tools can scale to meet the performance requirements of your application, especially for applications with high concurrency demands.
5. **Error Handling**: Evaluate how different tools handle errors, exceptions, and fault tolerance, especially in distributed systems.

6. **Community and Ecosystem**: Consider the availability of libraries, documentation, and community support for the chosen concurrency tools.

In conclusion, selecting the right concurrency tools is a critical decision in concurrent programming. Understanding your application's requirements and considering factors like language support, ease of use, scalability, error handling, and community support will help you make informed choices and build efficient concurrent applications.

Section 13.5: Testing Concurrent Code

Testing concurrent code presents unique challenges due to the inherent non-determinism and race conditions that can occur when multiple threads or processes execute concurrently. This section discusses strategies and techniques for effectively testing concurrent code to ensure its correctness and reliability.

The Importance of Concurrent Testing

Concurrent bugs are often elusive and hard to reproduce, making them particularly insidious. These bugs may only manifest under specific conditions or in rare edge cases, and they can lead to critical issues such as data corruption, deadlocks, or performance degradation. Therefore, thorough testing of concurrent code is essential to identify and address these issues before they impact production systems.

Strategies for Concurrent Testing

1. **Unit Testing**: Start with unit tests that focus on individual components of your concurrent code. Ensure that each

component behaves correctly in isolation. Mocking and stubbing can be valuable techniques to isolate units of code.

2. **Concurrency Frameworks**: Leverage concurrency testing frameworks designed for your programming language or platform. These frameworks provide tools for creating controlled concurrency scenarios and detecting race conditions.

3. **Randomized Testing**: Consider using randomized testing techniques, such as property-based testing (e.g., QuickCheck in Haskell), to explore a wide range of inputs and execution sequences. Randomized testing can reveal hidden concurrency issues.

4. **Deterministic Testing**: In cases where non-deterministic behavior is undesirable, use deterministic testing approaches. This involves carefully controlling the execution sequence of threads or processes to test specific scenarios.

5. **Code Review**: Conduct code reviews specifically focused on concurrent code. Multiple reviewers can help identify potential issues and suggest improvements.

6. **Static Analysis Tools**: Employ static analysis tools that can detect potential concurrency issues by analyzing your code without running it. These tools can catch data races, deadlocks, and other common concurrency problems.

Testing Tools and Frameworks

Several testing tools and frameworks are available to assist in testing concurrent code:

- **JUnit**: JUnit offers support for testing concurrent Java code with annotations like @Test and @RunWith.

- **JUnit Jupiter**: A more recent version of JUnit that provides improved support for concurrent testing.

- **TestNG**: A testing framework for Java that includes features for testing concurrent code.

- **Concurrency Stress Testing Libraries**: Libraries like Java's Jcstress[1] provide a way to stress-test the concurrency of your code, focusing on memory consistency and thread interaction.

- **Go Testing**: The Go programming language includes built-in support for testing concurrent code through goroutines and channels.

Testing Best Practices

When testing concurrent code, adhere to these best practices:

- **Isolation**: Ensure that tests are isolated from each other, and that each test leaves the system in a clean state to prevent interference between test cases.

- **Determinism**: Whenever possible, make tests deterministic. Non-deterministic tests can lead to unreliable test results.

- **Coverage**: Aim for comprehensive code coverage in your tests to increase the likelihood of catching concurrency-related issues.

- **Race Detection Tools**: Use race detection tools provided by your programming language or platform

---

1. https://openjdk.java.net/projects/code-tools/jcstress/

(e.g., Go's go test -race) to automatically detect race conditions.

- **Continuous Integration**: Incorporate concurrent tests into your continuous integration (CI) pipeline to identify issues early in the development process.

In conclusion, testing concurrent code requires a thoughtful approach, including unit testing, concurrency frameworks, randomized testing, and code reviews. By adopting the right testing tools and strategies, you can ensure the correctness and reliability of your concurrent applications, ultimately improving their quality and performance.

Chapter 14: Successive Refinement

In this chapter, we delve into the concept of successive refinement, a crucial practice in software development that involves iteratively improving the quality of your codebase. This process is akin to the sculpting of a work of art, where you start with a rough block and progressively refine it until it takes on a polished and elegant form. Successive refinement helps you enhance code clarity, maintainability, and functionality over time.

Section 14.1: The Process of Refining Code

Refining code is an essential aspect of producing clean and maintainable software. It involves a series of iterative steps aimed at enhancing different facets of your codebase. Here's an overview of the typical process of code refinement:

1. **Understand the Code**: Before you can refine code, you must thoroughly understand its purpose, functionality, and dependencies. Review any relevant documentation or

comments, and ensure you have a clear mental model of how the code works.

2. **Identify Areas for Improvement**: Carefully inspect the code to identify areas that require refinement. This could include improving code readability, removing redundancy, enhancing performance, or addressing bugs and design flaws.

3. **Set Clear Objectives**: Define clear objectives for the refinement process. What specific improvements are you aiming to achieve? Having well-defined goals will help you stay focused and measure the success of your efforts.

4. **Create a Plan**: Develop a plan that outlines the steps you'll take to refine the code. Consider breaking down the process into smaller tasks or issues that can be tackled one at a time.

5. **Prioritize Tasks**: Not all code improvements are equal in importance. Prioritize tasks based on their impact on the code's quality and functionality. High-priority issues, such as critical bugs, should be addressed first.

6. **Implement Changes**: Begin making changes to the code following the plan you've created. Be methodical and test your changes as you go to ensure they don't introduce new issues.

7. **Test Thoroughly**: After making changes, thoroughly test the code to verify that it still functions correctly and hasn't regressed in any way. Automated tests, if available, can be invaluable during this phase.

8. **Refactor**: In many cases, refinement involves refactoring—restructuring code to improve its organization and readability. Be prepared to refactor, but do so cautiously and with clear objectives in mind.

9. **Documentation**: Update documentation, comments, and

any relevant documentation to reflect the changes you've made. Clear and up-to-date documentation is vital for code maintainability.

10. **Review and Iterate**: After implementing changes, review the code again to ensure your objectives have been met. If additional improvements are necessary, iterate through the process again.

11. **Peer Review**: Consider involving colleagues or team members in a peer review process. Fresh perspectives can uncover issues you might have missed.

12. **Measure and Benchmark**: If performance improvements are part of your goals, measure and benchmark the code's performance before and after refinement to assess the impact of your changes.

13. **Document Decisions**: If you make significant decisions during the refinement process, document them. This can help future maintainers understand the rationale behind your changes.

14. **Celebrate Success**: Acknowledge and celebrate the successful refinement of code. Recognizing achievements can boost morale and motivate further improvements.

15. **Monitor and Maintain**: Even after refinement, continue to monitor the code for issues and be prepared to address them promptly. Maintenance is an ongoing process.

Successive refinement is not a one-time effort but an ongoing practice that should be integrated into your development workflow. By continuously improving your code, you can keep it clean, robust, and adaptable to changing requirements and technologies.

Section 14.2: Refactoring Techniques

Refactoring is a fundamental aspect of the successive refinement process. It involves restructuring code to enhance its clarity, maintainability, and efficiency without changing its external behavior. In this section, we'll explore some common refactoring techniques that you can apply to improve your code.

1. Extract Method

The Extract Method refactoring technique involves taking a block of code within a method and moving it into a separate method with a descriptive name. This can make the code more readable and modular. It's particularly useful when you have a complex or repetitive code block.

Before Refactoring:

```python
def calculate_total_price(cart):

total_price = 0

for item in cart:

subtotal = item['price'] * item['quantity']

total_price += subtotal

return total_price
```

After Refactoring:

```python
def calculate_total_price(cart):

total_price = 0

for item in cart:
```

```python
subtotal = calculate_subtotal(item)

total_price += subtotal

return total_price

def calculate_subtotal(item):

return item['price'] * item['quantity']
```

2. Rename Variables and Functions

Meaningful names are crucial for code readability. If you come across variables or functions with unclear or misleading names, rename them to reflect their purpose accurately.

Before Refactoring:

```python
def f(x):

result = 2 * x

return result
```

After Refactoring:

```python
def double(x):

doubled_value = 2 * x

return doubled_value
```

3. Remove Code Duplication

Code duplication should be minimized to improve maintainability and reduce the risk of bugs. Identify duplicated code segments and create reusable functions or classes to encapsulate them.

Before Refactoring:

```python
def calculate_area_of_rectangle(length, width):

area = length * width

return area

def calculate_area_of_square(side):

area = side * side

return area
```

After Refactoring:

```python
def calculate_area(length, width):

area = length * width

return area
```

4. Simplify Conditional Expressions

Complex conditional statements can be challenging to understand. Simplify them by using techniques like the ternary operator or breaking them into separate functions.

Before Refactoring:

```python
def get_discount(total_price, is_member):

if is_member:

if total_price > 100:

return 0.1

else:
```

return 0.05

else:

return 0.0

After Refactoring:

def get_discount(total_price, is_member):

if is_member **and** total_price > 100:

return 0.1

elif is_member:

return 0.05

else:

return 0.0

5. Encapsulate Conditional Logic

When you have conditional logic scattered throughout your code, encapsulate it within a function with a descriptive name. This makes the code more self-explanatory.

Before Refactoring:

if user_role == 'admin' **and** user_status == 'active' **and** user_age >= 18:

 # Perform admin actions

After Refactoring:

if is_admin(user_role, user_status, user_age):

 # Perform admin actions

def is_admin(role, status, age):

return role == 'admin' **and** status == 'active' **and** age >= 18

These are just a few examples of refactoring techniques that can significantly improve your code's quality. The key is to focus on enhancing readability, reducing complexity, and eliminating redundancy while ensuring that the code's behavior remains unchanged. Refactoring should be an integral part of your development process to maintain clean and maintainable code.

Section 14.3: Building Up Layers of Abstraction

In the pursuit of clean code, one of the essential principles is to build up layers of abstraction in your software. Abstraction involves hiding complex details behind simple and easily understandable interfaces. This approach improves the readability, maintainability, and scalability of your code. In this section, we'll delve into the importance of abstraction and how to create effective abstractions in your code.

Abstraction Benefits

1. **Readability**: Abstraction allows you to represent complex operations or concepts with concise, high-level functions or classes. This makes your code more readable and understandable, even for developers who are not intimately familiar with the underlying implementation.
2. **Maintainability**: By encapsulating details within abstractions, you can modify the implementation without affecting the code that uses the abstraction. This reduces

the risk of introducing bugs when making changes.

3. **Scalability**: Abstraction provides a foundation for extending your codebase. You can add new features or functionalities without disrupting existing code, as long as the interface remains consistent.

Creating Abstractions

Creating effective abstractions requires thoughtful design and adherence to certain principles:

1. **Single Responsibility Principle (SRP)**: Each abstraction, whether it's a class or a function, should have a single, well-defined responsibility. This ensures that your abstractions remain focused and easy to understand.
2. **Interface Design**: Define clear and intuitive interfaces for your abstractions. These interfaces should provide all necessary operations while hiding implementation details. Well-designed interfaces are crucial for clean code.
3. **Encapsulation**: Hide internal details and implementation complexities. Expose only what's necessary for the user of the abstraction. This reduces the cognitive load when working with the code.

Example of Abstraction

Let's consider an example where we want to abstract away the process of sending notifications via different channels (e.g., email, SMS, push notification). We can create an abstraction called NotificationService:

```python
class NotificationService:

    def send_notification(self, message, recipient):
```

```python
pass

class EmailNotificationService(NotificationService):

def send_notification(self, message, recipient):

# Implementation for sending email notification

class SMSNotificationService(NotificationService):

def send_notification(self, message, recipient):

# Implementation for sending SMS notification

class PushNotificationService(NotificationService):

def send_notification(self, message, recipient):

# Implementation for sending push notification
```

In this example, NotificationService is an abstraction that defines the interface for sending notifications. Concrete implementations like EmailNotificationService, SMSNotificationService, and PushNotificationService provide the specific implementation details for each channel.

By using this abstraction, you can easily switch between notification channels without affecting the code that uses the NotificationService interface. This demonstrates how abstraction simplifies code management and enhances flexibility.

Conclusion

Building up layers of abstraction is a crucial aspect of clean code development. It promotes readability, maintainability, and scalability while allowing you to manage complexity effectively. By adhering to principles like SRP, interface design, and encapsulation, you can create meaningful abstractions that contribute to clean and maintainable code.

Section 14.4: The Importance of Communication

Clean code development is not just about writing code that the computer can understand; it's also about writing code that other developers can understand. Effective communication among team members is essential for creating and maintaining clean code. In this section, we'll explore the importance of communication in clean code practices.

Code as a Communication Medium

Code is a form of communication between developers. It conveys your intentions, decisions, and solutions to specific problems. Therefore, it's crucial to write code that clearly communicates your thought process to others. Clean code prioritizes human readability and comprehension.

Writing Self-Explanatory Code

One way to facilitate effective communication through code is to make your code self-explanatory. Self-explanatory code is easy to understand without requiring extensive comments or documentation. This can be achieved through meaningful variable and function names, clear organization, and consistent coding conventions.

Consider the following code snippet:

```
# Non-self-explanatory code

if d == 1:
```

```
t = 60 * s
```

else:

```
t = (s * 60) / d
```

In the above code, it's not immediately clear what d and s represent or what the calculation is meant to achieve. A cleaner and more self-explanatory version might look like this:

 # Self-explanatory code

if is_direct_route:

```
travel_time_minutes = distance_miles * 60 / speed_mph
```

else:

```
travel_time_minutes = (distance_miles * 60) / (speed_mph * detour_factor)
```

In the improved version, variable names are chosen to describe their purpose, and comments are avoided by using expressive code.

Collaborative Development

Clean code practices encourage collaboration among team members. When everyone adheres to consistent coding styles, naming conventions, and documentation standards, it becomes easier for multiple developers to work together efficiently. Clean code emphasizes the importance of code reviews and discussions, which help catch issues early and improve code quality.

Documentation and Comments

While clean code aims to make code as self-explanatory as possible, there are cases where documentation and comments are still necessary. These include explaining complex algorithms, design decisions, or providing context for unusual solutions. However, comments should complement clean code rather than substitute for it. They should be kept up to date and be used sparingly.

Conclusion

Effective communication among developers is a cornerstone of clean code development. Writing self-explanatory code, following coding conventions, and encouraging collaboration lead to code that is not only functional but also understandable by others. By prioritizing communication, clean code practices make software development more efficient and maintainable for teams.

Section 14.5: Code Clarity Through Refinement

Refinement is a fundamental concept in clean code development. It refers to the process of continually improving code by making it clearer, more maintainable, and more efficient. This section explores how refinement contributes to code clarity and overall code quality.

The Continuous Improvement Cycle

Clean code is not a one-time effort but an ongoing process of refinement. Developers should strive to improve their code continuously, even after it's initially written. This involves revisiting code, identifying areas for enhancement, and making incremental changes.

Refinement follows a cycle that includes the following steps:

1. **Identify Improvement Opportunities:** Start by identifying areas of your codebase that can be improved.

This could be based on code reviews, feedback from team members, or your own observations.

2. **Plan and Prioritize:** Once you've identified areas for improvement, create a plan to address them. Prioritize changes based on their impact on code quality and maintainability.

3. **Make Incremental Changes:** Instead of attempting large-scale refactoring, make small, incremental changes to avoid introducing bugs or destabilizing the codebase. Each change should have a clear objective, such as improving readability or reducing duplication.

4. **Test and Validate:** After making changes, thoroughly test the code to ensure it still functions correctly. Automated tests, such as unit tests, can help catch regressions.

5. **Document and Communicate:** If your changes affect the behavior of the code or its usage, update documentation and communicate these changes to the team.

6. **Review and Iterate:** Collaborate with team members to review the changes and gather feedback. Iteratively refine the code based on this feedback.

Code Clarity Goals

The primary goal of refinement is to enhance code clarity. Clear code is easier to read, understand, and maintain. When code is clear, developers can quickly grasp its purpose and make modifications with confidence. Here are some common aspects of code clarity that refinement aims to achieve:

- **Simplicity:** Strive for simplicity in your code. Complex solutions should be simplified, and convoluted logic should be refactored into clearer alternatives.

- **Modularity:** Break down large and monolithic code into smaller, modular components. This enhances code organization and makes it easier to reason about.

- **Naming and Documentation:** Pay attention to variable and function names. Choose names that accurately describe their purpose. Documentation, such as comments and README files, should also be clear and up-to-date.

- **Reduction of Duplication:** Eliminate code duplication wherever possible. Repeated code segments should be abstracted into reusable functions or classes.

- **Consistency:** Maintain consistent coding style and conventions throughout the codebase. Inconsistent code can confuse developers and lead to errors.

Balancing Refinement

While refinement is essential, it should be balanced with pragmatism. Not all code requires constant refinement, and not all improvements are equally valuable. Prioritize refinement efforts based on the specific needs of your project and team.

In conclusion, refinement plays a vital role in achieving code clarity in clean code development. By following a continuous improvement cycle and focusing on clarity goals, developers can create and maintain code that is understandable, maintainable, and of high quality. Refinement is not a one-time activity but a discipline that contributes to the long-term success of a software project.

Chapter 15: JUnit Internals

Section 15.1: Examining the JUnit Framework

JUnit is a widely used testing framework for Java that simplifies the process of writing and executing unit tests. It provides a set of annotations and classes to define and run tests, making it an essential tool for test-driven development (TDD) and ensuring the correctness of your code.

Understanding the JUnit Framework

JUnit follows a simple and effective testing pattern. Here are some key components and concepts within the JUnit framework:

1. **Test Cases**: In JUnit, test cases are represented as methods within a test class. These methods are annotated with @Test to indicate that they are test methods.
2. **Assertions**: JUnit provides a variety of assertion methods (e.g., assertEquals, assertTrue, assertNotNull) to validate the expected outcomes of your code. If an assertion fails, the test case is marked as a failure.
3. **Test Runners**: JUnit uses test runners to execute test cases. The most common test runner is JUnitCore, which can be used to run tests from the command line.
4. **Test Suites**: Test suites allow you to group related test cases into a single suite. This can be useful for organizing and executing multiple tests together.
5. **Annotations**: JUnit uses annotations to define test methods and perform setup and teardown tasks. Common annotations include @Test, @Before, @After,

@BeforeClass, and @AfterClass.

6. **Fixtures**: JUnit allows you to set up and tear down common resources or states before and after test execution using the @Before and @After annotations. This helps ensure that each test starts with a consistent environment.

Writing a Simple JUnit Test

Let's take a look at a basic example of writing a JUnit test:

```java
import org.junit.Test;

import static org.junit.Assert.*;

public class MyMathTest {

@Test

public void testAddition() {

int result = MyMath.add(2, 3);

assertEquals(5, result);

}

}
```

In this example:

- We import the necessary JUnit classes and methods.

- We create a test class called MyMathTest.

- Inside the class, we define a test method testAddition. This method is annotated with @Test to indicate that it's a test case.

- Inside the test method, we use assertions like assertEquals to check if the result of the add method matches our expectations.

Running JUnit Tests

You can run JUnit tests using various tools and IDEs. One common way is to use the JUnitCore runner from the command line. For example:

```
java -cp junit.jar:. org.junit.runner.JUnitCore MyMathTest
```

This command runs the MyMathTest class using JUnitCore. The classpath (-cp) includes the JUnit library (junit.jar) and the current directory (.).

JUnit provides rich functionality for testing, including parameterized tests, test suites, and mocking. Understanding the internals of JUnit helps you write effective and maintainable unit tests for your Java applications. In the following sections, we'll explore more about writing testable code and common testing patterns.

In the next section, we'll delve into implementing your own test framework, which will provide you with insights into how testing frameworks like JUnit work under the hood.

Section 15.2: Implementing Your Own Test Framework

While JUnit is a powerful and widely-used testing framework, understanding how it works under the hood can be beneficial for improving your testing skills and even for building custom testing solutions when needed. In this section, we'll explore the process of implementing a simple test framework to gain insights into the inner workings of testing frameworks like JUnit.

The Basic Structure of a Test Framework

A test framework typically consists of several key components:

1. **Test Runner**: The test runner is responsible for discovering and executing test cases. It identifies test classes and their methods, runs the tests, and reports the results.
2. **Annotations**: Annotations are used to mark test methods, setup and teardown methods, and other special methods. They provide metadata to the test runner.
3. **Test Execution**: The test runner executes test methods in a specified order, typically following a naming convention or other rules.
4. **Assertions**: Assertions are used within test methods to check if a condition is true. If an assertion fails, the test case is marked as a failure.
5. **Reporting**: The test framework should generate reports that summarize the results of test execution, indicating which tests passed and which failed.

A Minimal Test Framework in Java

Here's a simplified example of a test framework in Java:

```java
import java.util.ArrayList;

import java.util.List;

public class SimpleTestFramework {

private static List<String> failedTests = new ArrayList<>();
```

```java
public static void main(String[] args) {

runTests();

printResults();

}

public static void runTests() {

runTest("Test 1", () -> assertEquals(2 + 2, 4));

runTest("Test 2", () -> assertEquals(3 * 3, 9));

}

public static void runTest(String testName, Runnable test) {

try {

test.run();

System.out.println(testName + " - Passed");

} catch (AssertionError e) {

failedTests.add(testName);

System.err.println(testName + " - Failed: " + e.getMessage());

}

}

public static void assertEquals(int actual, int expected) {

if (actual != expected) {

throw new AssertionError("Expected " + expected + ", but got " +
actual);
```

```java
}

}

public static void printResults() {

if (failedTests.isEmpty()) {

System.out.println("All tests passed!");

} else {

System.out.println("Failed tests:");

for (String testName : failedTests) {

System.out.println(testName);

}

}

}

}
```

In this simplified example:

- We define a SimpleTestFramework class with methods for running tests, asserting equality, and printing results.

- The runTests method runs two test cases, and each test case is defined as a lambda expression.

- If an assertion fails, an AssertionError is thrown and caught, and the test is marked as failed.

- Finally, we print the results, indicating which tests passed and which failed.

Building a Full-Fledged Test Framework

Real-world test frameworks like JUnit are more complex and feature-rich than this minimal example. They support features like parameterized tests, test suites, and sophisticated reporting. However, this simple framework illustrates the fundamental concepts of a test framework and how tests can be executed and reported.

By understanding these basics, you'll be better equipped to write effective unit tests, troubleshoot testing issues, and appreciate the convenience of mature testing frameworks like JUnit.

Section 15.3: Writing Testable Code

Writing testable code is a fundamental practice in software development. Testable code is code that can be easily tested using unit tests, making it more reliable and maintainable. In this section, we'll explore the principles and techniques for writing code that is conducive to testing.

The Importance of Testable Code

Testable code offers several benefits:

1. **Bug Detection**: Unit tests can help identify bugs and regressions early in the development process, reducing the cost of fixing issues later.
2. **Documentation**: Tests serve as documentation for how the code is expected to behave. They provide clear examples of how to use the code.

3. **Refactoring Confidence**: With tests in place, you can confidently refactor or modify code to improve its design without fear of introducing defects.

4. **Collaboration**: Testable code encourages collaboration among team members, as they can work on different parts of the codebase while relying on tests to maintain correctness.

Principles of Writing Testable Code

To write testable code, consider the following principles:

1. Separation of Concerns (SoC)

Divide your code into small, focused modules or functions, each with a single responsibility. This makes it easier to write tests for individual components.

2. Dependency Injection

Avoid hardcoding dependencies within your code. Instead, inject dependencies (e.g., via constructor injection or method parameters) to make it easier to provide mock objects for testing.

3. Favor Composition over Inheritance

Prefer composition to inheritance to achieve code reuse. This allows you to compose objects with specific behaviors, making it easier to substitute implementations for testing.

4. Keep State External

Minimize mutable internal state. Favor immutability and keep state external (e.g., in parameters or dependencies) to ensure that functions and methods are pure and deterministic.

5. Avoid Global State

Avoid reliance on global variables or singletons, as they can make it challenging to isolate and test components.

6. Encapsulate Complexity

Complex logic should be encapsulated within functions or classes with well-defined interfaces. This simplifies testing and improves code readability.

7. Use Interfaces and Abstraction

Use interfaces and abstractions to define contracts between components. This allows you to create mock implementations for testing.

Writing Testable Code Example

Let's consider a simple example in Java to illustrate writing testable code:

```java
public class Calculator {

public int add(int a, int b) {

return a + b;
```

```java
}

public int divide(int dividend, int divisor) {

if (divisor == 0) {

throw new IllegalArgumentException("Divisor cannot be zero.");

}

return dividend / divisor;

}

}
```

This Calculator class provides two methods, add and divide. To make it more testable:

- We've kept the methods small and focused.

- We've encapsulated error handling for division by zero.

- We haven't relied on global state.

With these principles in mind, we can easily write unit tests for the Calculator class to ensure that it behaves correctly in various scenarios.

In conclusion, writing testable code is an essential practice for building robust software. By following the principles of separation of concerns, dependency injection, and encapsulation, among others, you can create code that is easier to test, maintain, and evolve over time.

Section 15.4: The Role of Test Automation

Test automation plays a crucial role in modern software development. It involves the use of automated scripts and tools to execute tests, validate software functionality, and identify defects quickly. In this section, we will explore the significance of test automation and how it contributes to the quality of software.

Benefits of Test Automation

Test automation offers several benefits that significantly impact the software development process:

1. **Efficiency**: Automated tests can be executed quickly and repetitively, saving time compared to manual testing. This efficiency is essential, especially in agile development environments with frequent releases.
2. **Accuracy**: Automated tests execute test cases with precision, reducing the likelihood of human errors in testing. This leads to more reliable test results.
3. **Reusability**: Test automation allows for the creation of reusable test suites. Once a test is automated, it can be rerun whenever needed, ensuring consistent and repeatable testing.
4. **Regression Testing**: Automated tests excel at regression testing. Whenever code changes occur, regression tests can quickly identify if existing functionality is affected.
5. **Parallel Testing**: Automation enables parallel execution of tests on multiple configurations and platforms, reducing the overall testing time.
6. **Continuous Integration (CI)**: Test automation integrates seamlessly with CI/CD pipelines, automatically running tests with each code commit. This ensures that new code

changes do not introduce regressions.

Types of Automated Tests

Various types of automated tests can be employed during the software development lifecycle:

1. **Unit Tests**: These focus on testing individual units of code, such as functions or methods, in isolation. Unit tests are typically written by developers and help ensure that each piece of code functions correctly.
2. **Integration Tests**: Integration tests verify the interaction between different components or modules of a system. They ensure that these components work together as expected.
3. **Functional Tests**: Functional tests assess the software's functionality from an end-user perspective. They validate that the software meets the specified requirements.
4. **Regression Tests**: Regression tests confirm that new code changes have not introduced defects or caused existing functionality to break.
5. **Performance Tests**: Performance tests evaluate the system's speed, responsiveness, and scalability under different load conditions.
6. **Security Tests**: Security tests identify vulnerabilities and weaknesses in the software's security mechanisms. They help protect against security threats.

Test Automation Tools

Several test automation tools and frameworks are available, catering to different programming languages and technologies. Some popular ones include:

- **JUnit**: A widely used testing framework for Java.

- **Selenium**: A tool for automating web browser interactions.

- **PyTest**: A Python-based testing framework.

- **Cypress**: An end-to-end testing framework for web applications.

- **JUnit**: A popular testing framework for JavaScript.

- **Postman**: An API testing tool.

- **Jenkins**: A CI/CD automation server with test execution capabilities.

The choice of tool depends on the project's requirements, technology stack, and team's expertise.

Challenges in Test Automation

While test automation offers numerous advantages, it also presents challenges:

1. **Initial Setup**: Setting up automation frameworks and scripts requires time and effort.
2. **Maintenance**: Automated tests need regular updates to accommodate changes in the application or requirements.
3. **Test Data**: Managing test data for automation can be complex, especially for scenarios involving large datasets.
4. **Flakiness**: Some automated tests may produce inconsistent results due to factors like environment variability or timing issues.
5. **Skill Requirements**: Team members need training and

expertise in automation tools and frameworks.

Conclusion

Test automation is a critical component of modern software development. It enhances efficiency, accuracy, and reliability in testing, contributing to the delivery of high-quality software. By choosing the right types of tests, automation tools, and addressing challenges effectively, development teams can harness the full potential of test automation in their projects.

Section 15.5: Test Smells and Refactoring Tests

In the world of software development, where code quality is paramount, even your tests should be well-structured and maintainable. Test code, like production code, can suffer from various issues referred to as "test smells." Just as you refactor your production code to improve its quality, you should also refactor your tests to ensure they remain effective and maintainable over time.

Understanding Test Smells

Test smells are patterns or anti-patterns that indicate issues with your test code. Recognizing these smells is crucial for keeping your test suite healthy. Some common test smells include:

1. **Fragile Tests**: Tests that frequently break due to minor changes in the production code. Fragile tests are a sign of tight coupling between tests and code, which should be avoided.

2. **Flaky Tests**: Tests that produce inconsistent results, sometimes passing and sometimes failing, without changes in the code. Flakiness often indicates issues with test

isolation or external dependencies.

3. **Overly Complex Tests**: Tests that are overly complicated, making them hard to understand and maintain. They might include unnecessary setup or too many assertions.
4. **Duplicate Tests**: Having multiple tests that cover the same scenario can lead to redundancy and maintenance challenges.
5. **Slow Tests**: Tests that take a long time to run can slow down the development process. Slow tests discourage frequent test execution, which can lead to problems going unnoticed.
6. **Lack of Isolation**: Tests that rely on shared global state or depend on the execution order of other tests can lead to issues when tests are run in isolation.

Refactoring Tests

Refactoring tests involves improving their structure and maintainability while preserving their correctness. Here are some techniques to address test smells:

1. **Separate Concerns**: Ensure that test setup, execution, and verification are cleanly separated within each test case. Use appropriate fixtures and arrange-act-assert (AAA) patterns.
2. **Avoid Code Duplication**: If you find multiple tests with similar setup, consider creating a test utility or helper methods to reduce duplication.
3. **Use Test Data Builders**: When creating complex test data, consider using test data builders to make test setup more readable and maintainable.
4. **Reduce Test Dependencies**: Isolate tests by avoiding unnecessary dependencies on other tests or global state. Use mocks or stubs to replace real dependencies when

needed.

5. **Mock External Dependencies**: When dealing with external services or resources, use mocking frameworks to control their behavior during tests. This reduces test flakiness.

6. **Parallelize Tests**: When possible, parallelize test execution to reduce overall test time. This can encourage more frequent testing.

7. **Refactor Slow Tests**: Identify and optimize slow tests to reduce their execution time. Consider using techniques like test doubles (e.g., fakes or spies) to speed up tests.

8. **Automate Test Execution**: Implement automated test execution as part of your CI/CD pipeline. This ensures that tests are run consistently with every code change.

Continuous Improvement

Refactoring tests is an ongoing process. As your codebase evolves, regularly review and improve your tests. Encourage team members to follow testing best practices and maintain a high standard for test quality.

Remember that well-structured tests not only help catch defects early but also serve as documentation for your code. Clean and maintainable tests contribute to the overall health of your software and the efficiency of your development process.

In conclusion, test smells are indicators of issues in your test suite. Refactoring tests, just like refactoring production code, is essential to maintain a robust and efficient testing environment. By addressing test smells and continuously improving your testing practices, you can ensure that your tests remain a valuable asset throughout the software development lifecycle.

Chapter 16: Refactoring SerialDate

In this chapter, we will delve into a real-life refactoring example to demonstrate the principles of clean code and the refactoring process. Refactoring is an essential practice for improving the quality of existing code while preserving its behavior. By the end of this chapter, you will have a better understanding of how to identify problems in code, plan refactoring steps, and reap the benefits of clean code.

Section 16.1: Real-Life Refactoring Example

To illustrate the concepts of clean code and refactoring, let's consider a practical scenario involving a class called SerialDate. This class represents dates in a non-standard serialization format, and it suffers from various code quality issues and design problems. Our goal is to refactor this class to make it more maintainable, readable, and aligned with clean code principles.

Analyzing SerialDate's Problems

Before we begin refactoring, it's crucial to analyze the existing code and identify its problems. Here are some of the issues with the current implementation of SerialDate:

1. **Large and Complex Methods**: The class contains large and complex methods, making it challenging to understand and maintain.
2. **Lack of Modularity**: The code lacks modularity and separation of concerns. There is no clear organization of functionality.
3. **Inconsistent Naming**: Inconsistent naming conventions make it hard to understand variable and method names.

4. **Low Testability**: The code is difficult to test due to tight coupling and a lack of proper abstractions.
5. **Inefficient Data Structures**: The class uses inefficient data structures for date calculations.

The Refactoring Process

The refactoring process involves making incremental changes to improve the code's structure and readability. Here are the general steps we will follow:

1. **Identify Smells**: We have already identified some code smells in SerialDate. During the initial analysis, we will pinpoint additional issues.
2. **Create Tests**: Before making changes, we will create a comprehensive test suite for SerialDate to ensure that its behavior remains consistent after refactoring.
3. **Plan Refactoring Steps**: We will plan the refactoring steps, breaking down the process into smaller, manageable tasks.
4. **Refactor Incrementally**: We will refactor the code incrementally, focusing on one issue at a time. After each change, we will run the tests to ensure that we haven't introduced regressions.
5. **Maintain Documentation**: As we refactor, we will update comments and documentation to reflect the new code structure.
6. **Measure and Validate**: We will measure the code's improved maintainability and validate that it adheres to clean code principles.

Incremental Refactoring Steps

Throughout this chapter, we will demonstrate a series of incremental refactoring steps applied to SerialDate. These steps will address various code smells and design issues. By the end, you will witness the transformation of a problematic class into a clean and well-structured one.

Refactoring is an iterative and continuous process that pays off by making the codebase more maintainable and adaptable to changing requirements. It is an essential skill for any software developer and is closely tied to the principles of clean code.

In the following sections, we will dive into the first steps of the refactoring process and begin the transformation of SerialDate.

Section 16.2: Analyzing SerialDate's Problems

In the previous section, we introduced the real-life refactoring example involving the SerialDate class. To proceed with the refactoring process effectively, it's crucial to perform a detailed analysis of the existing code. This step will help us identify specific issues, code smells, and design problems that need to be addressed. Let's dive deeper into the analysis of SerialDate:

1. Large and Complex Methods

One of the most noticeable issues with SerialDate is the presence of large and complex methods. These methods are responsible for various date-related calculations and formatting, making them challenging to understand and maintain. The code's lack of modularity and organization exacerbates this problem.

To address this issue, we will aim to break down these large methods into smaller, more focused functions. This practice aligns with the clean code principle of having small and focused functions.

2. Lack of Modularity

The existing code lacks modularity and separation of concerns. Date-related functionality, such as parsing, formatting, and calculations, is intermingled within the same methods. This lack of clear organization makes it difficult to reason about the code's behavior and maintainability.

Our refactoring efforts will involve restructuring the code to introduce clear modules or classes responsible for specific aspects of date handling. This separation of concerns enhances code maintainability and readability.

3. Inconsistent Naming

Inconsistent naming conventions within the SerialDate class contribute to code readability issues. Variable and method names are not uniform, making it challenging to understand their purposes and intentions.

During the refactoring process, we will focus on improving naming conventions, ensuring that names are descriptive and follow a consistent style. Clear and meaningful names are a fundamental aspect of clean code.

4. Low Testability

The current design of SerialDate makes it challenging to test in isolation. Tight coupling between methods and a lack of proper abstractions hinder unit testing efforts. To address this issue, we will introduce abstractions and refactor the code to improve testability.

5. Inefficient Data Structures

The code uses inefficient data structures and algorithms for date calculations. This inefficiency can impact performance and maintainability. As part of our refactoring, we will evaluate and replace these data structures with more suitable alternatives.

In summary, the analysis of SerialDate reveals several critical issues related to code structure, modularity, naming, testability, and algorithmic efficiency. In the subsequent sections of this chapter, we will tackle these issues one by one, demonstrating the steps taken to transform SerialDate into a clean and maintainable class. Refactoring is an iterative process, and each step contributes to the overall improvement of the codebase.

Section 16.3: The Refactoring Process

Now that we've identified the issues and challenges within the SerialDate class, it's time to embark on the refactoring journey. Refactoring is a systematic process of restructuring existing code to improve its readability, maintainability, and extensibility without changing its external behavior. In this section, we will outline the key steps involved in the refactoring process for SerialDate.

1. Create a Test Suite

Before making any changes to the code, it's essential to establish a comprehensive test suite. This suite will serve as a safety net, ensuring that our refactoring efforts do not introduce new defects. We will write unit tests for the existing functionality of SerialDate, covering various edge cases and scenarios.

2. Identify and Isolate Concerns

One of the primary goals of refactoring is to improve code modularity and separation of concerns. We will start by identifying distinct concerns within the SerialDate class, such as parsing, formatting, and date calculations. Each concern will be isolated into its own module or class, adhering to the Single Responsibility Principle (SRP).

3. Extract Small, Focused Functions

The large and complex methods in the original SerialDate class will be refactored into smaller, focused functions. Each function will have a clear and single responsibility, making the code easier to understand and maintain. This aligns with the principle of small and focused functions.

4. Improve Naming and Documentation

Inconsistent and unclear naming conventions will be addressed during the refactoring process. We will ensure that variable and method names are descriptive, meaningful, and follow a consistent style. Additionally, we will update or provide documentation to clarify the purpose and usage of various components.

5. Enhance Testability

To facilitate effective unit testing, we will introduce abstractions and interfaces where necessary. This will enable us to mock dependencies and isolate components for testing purposes. The goal is to make the codebase more testable and robust.

6. Replace Inefficient Data Structures and Algorithms

Any inefficient data structures or algorithms used for date calculations will be replaced with more efficient alternatives. This will improve both the performance and maintainability of the code.

7. Continuous Testing and Validation

Throughout the refactoring process, we will continuously run the test suite to validate that the code's behavior remains consistent. Any deviations from the expected behavior will be addressed promptly.

8. Incremental Refactoring

Refactoring is an iterative process, and we will perform it incrementally, focusing on one concern or module at a time. This approach minimizes the risk of introducing errors and allows us to maintain a stable codebase throughout the process.

9. Code Review and Collaboration

If applicable, code reviews and collaboration with team members can be beneficial during the refactoring process. Different perspectives and insights can lead to better solutions and cleaner code.

10. Measure Progress

As we refactor SerialDate, it's essential to measure our progress in terms of code quality, readability, and maintainability. Tools and metrics can help assess the impact of our changes.

In conclusion, the refactoring process for SerialDate will involve a series of deliberate and well-planned steps aimed at transforming the existing code into clean and maintainable software. Each step contributes to the overall improvement of the codebase, ensuring that it aligns with the principles of clean code and software craftsmanship.

Section 16.4: Incremental Refactoring Steps

Refactoring the SerialDate class involves a series of incremental steps that gradually transform the existing code into a cleaner and more maintainable state. In this section, we will outline these incremental refactoring steps, keeping in mind the overarching goal of improving the code's structure and readability.

Step 1: Create a Test Suite

Before making any changes to the code, we create a comprehensive test suite for the SerialDate class. This suite includes unit tests that cover various aspects of the class's functionality. The goal is to ensure that our refactoring efforts do not introduce defects or alter the external behavior of the class.

Step 2: Isolate Parsing Logic

The first concern we address is the parsing of serial dates from strings. We create a new class or module dedicated to parsing logic, adhering to the Single Responsibility Principle (SRP). This separation of concerns makes the code more modular and easier to understand.

Step 3: Refactor Date Calculation Methods

The date calculation methods within the SerialDate class are often large and complex. We begin by refactoring these methods into smaller, focused functions. Each function is responsible for a specific date calculation, improving readability and maintainability.

Step 4: Improve Naming and Documentation

In this step, we focus on improving the naming of variables, methods, and classes. Descriptive and meaningful names make the code self-explanatory. Additionally, we provide or update documentation to clarify the purpose and usage of various components.

Step 5: Extract Formatting Logic

Formatting of serial dates is another concern that needs attention. We isolate the formatting logic into its own module or class, following the SRP. This separation allows for better code organization and easier future changes.

Step 6: Enhance Testability

To facilitate unit testing, we introduce abstractions and interfaces where necessary. This enables us to mock dependencies and isolate components for testing purposes. Ensuring the code is testable is a critical aspect of the refactoring process.

Step 7: Replace Inefficient Algorithms

Any inefficient algorithms or data structures used for date calculations are replaced with more efficient alternatives. This step focuses on improving both performance and code quality.

Step 8: Continuous Testing and Validation

Throughout the entire refactoring process, we continuously run the test suite to validate that the code's behavior remains consistent. Any regressions or unexpected behavior are addressed promptly.

Step 9: Incremental and Iterative

Refactoring is an iterative process. We apply the above steps incrementally, one concern or module at a time. This approach minimizes the risk of introducing errors and ensures a stable codebase throughout the process.

Step 10: Code Review and Collaboration

Collaboration with team members and code reviews, if applicable, can provide valuable insights and ensure that the refactoring efforts align with the project's goals and coding standards.

Step 11: Measure Progress

Throughout the refactoring process, we use tools and metrics to measure progress in terms of code quality, readability, and maintainability. This data helps assess the impact of our changes and guides further improvements.

By following these incremental steps, we transform the SerialDate class from its initial state into clean and maintainable code. The process is deliberate, systematic, and focused on preserving the functionality of the class while enhancing its structure and readability.

Section 16.5: The Benefits of Clean Code

Throughout the refactoring journey of the SerialDate class, we have discussed various techniques and principles for transforming messy, hard-to-maintain code into clean code. Clean code is not just an abstract concept; it brings concrete benefits to software development projects and the developers themselves.

1. Improved Readability

Clean code is highly readable and easy to understand. When you or other developers revisit the code, you can quickly grasp its intent and functionality. This reduces the time required for code reviews, debugging, and maintenance.

2. Enhanced Maintainability

Maintaining code is a significant part of the software development lifecycle. Clean code is modular, well-organized, and follows best practices. It makes maintenance tasks, such as adding features or fixing bugs, more straightforward and less error-prone.

3. Reduced Technical Debt

Technical debt accumulates when shortcuts are taken or code quality is compromised. Clean code minimizes technical debt by emphasizing quality from the start. This reduces the risk of future rework and refactoring.

4. Easier Collaboration

Clean code is a common language that all team members can understand. It fosters collaboration by enabling developers to work seamlessly on shared codebases. Code reviews and pair programming become more productive.

5. Better Debugging

Clean code exhibits fewer defects, and when issues arise, they are easier to locate and fix. Debugging becomes less of a time-consuming process because clean code is well-structured and logically organized.

6. Increased Developer Productivity

Developers spend less time deciphering complex code and more time building new features or optimizing existing ones. This boosts overall productivity and project efficiency.

7. Code Reusability

Clean code often results in modular components that can be reused across different parts of the project or in other projects entirely. This reusability reduces duplication of effort and improves consistency.

8. Confidence in Changes

With clean code, you can confidently make changes or refactor without fear of unintended consequences. Comprehensive test coverage ensures that modifications don't introduce regressions.

9. Enhanced Documentation

Clean code promotes good documentation practices. Developers are more likely to provide clear comments, meaningful variable names, and up-to-date documentation, which benefits both current and future contributors.

10. Long-Term Cost Savings

While clean code requires an initial investment in terms of time and effort, it pays off over the long term. Reduced maintenance costs, faster development cycles, and fewer defects translate into cost savings for the project.

11. Developer Satisfaction

Developers take pride in writing clean, maintainable code. It fosters a sense of ownership and satisfaction in their work. High code quality contributes to a positive working environment.

12. Software Resilience

Clean code is robust and resilient to changes. It can adapt to evolving requirements and technologies, ensuring the software's longevity.

In summary, the benefits of clean code extend far beyond just aesthetics. Clean code is a cornerstone of successful software development projects. It empowers developers, enhances collaboration, reduces risk, and ultimately delivers higher-quality software to users. Embracing clean code principles is an investment that pays dividends throughout the software's lifecycle.

Chapter 17: Smells and Heuristics

Section 17.1: Recognizing Code Smells

Code smells are specific patterns or characteristics in code that indicate potential problems or areas for improvement. They are not bugs but rather indications of areas where the code may not be as clean or maintainable as it could be. Recognizing code smells is an essential skill for developers, as it can lead to more effective refactoring and overall code improvement. In this section, we'll explore various common code smells and how to identify them.

1. Duplicated Code (DRY Violation)

Duplicated code occurs when the same or very similar code appears in multiple places within a codebase. This redundancy can lead to maintenance challenges because changes must be made in multiple locations.

2. Long Methods

Long methods contain a large number of lines of code, making them challenging to understand and maintain. They often indicate that a method is responsible for too many things.

3. Large Classes

Large classes have too many responsibilities and methods, violating the Single Responsibility Principle (SRP). They can be difficult to comprehend and maintain.

4. Complex Conditional Logic

Code with deeply nested if statements, complex boolean expressions, or excessive switch/case statements can be challenging to follow and test. It's a sign that the code's logic might need simplification.

5. Inconsistent Naming

Inconsistent naming conventions for variables, functions, or classes can lead to confusion. Code should follow a consistent naming style that reflects its purpose.

6. Comments as a Crutch

Excessive comments can indicate that the code is not self-explanatory. While comments are essential for clarifying complex logic, code should ideally be self-documenting through well-named variables and functions.

7. Feature Envy

Feature envy occurs when a method in one class accesses the data or methods of another class excessively. It suggests that the method might belong in the other class or that there's a better way to structure the code.

8. Long Parameter Lists

Methods with many parameters can be hard to use and maintain. They might indicate that a class is trying to do too much, and some of its responsibilities should be moved elsewhere.

9. Data Clumps

Data clumps are groups of data that appear together throughout the code. It can indicate that these data items should be encapsulated in a separate class or structure.

10. Switch Statements

Repeated switch statements based on the same condition are a sign of a missed opportunity for polymorphism. They can often be replaced with a more object-oriented approach using inheritance and interfaces.

11. Mutable Data

Overuse of mutable data can lead to unexpected side effects and bugs. Immutability and functional programming principles can provide more predictable code.

12. Lazy Class

A lazy class is one that doesn't do much and doesn't contribute significantly to the codebase. Removing or refactoring such classes can simplify the codebase.

Recognizing these code smells is just the first step. Once identified, developers can use various refactoring techniques to address them and improve the quality of the code. Code review and collaboration among team members are valuable for identifying and addressing code smells effectively.

Section 17.2: Common Code Smells and Solutions

In the previous section, we discussed how to recognize code smells—indicators of potential issues in code. Now, let's delve deeper into some common code smells and explore solutions for each of them. Addressing these code smells can lead to cleaner, more maintainable code.

Duplicated Code (DRY Violation)

Symptom: The same or very similar code appears in multiple places within the codebase.

Solution: Extract the duplicated code into a reusable function, method, or class. By doing so, you follow the DRY (Don't Repeat

Yourself) principle, making it easier to maintain and update the code in one place. Additionally, consider using inheritance, interfaces, or composition to share common behavior across classes.

```
# Before refactoring

def calculate_area_of_square(side_length):

return side_length * side_length

def calculate_area_of_rectangle(length, width):

return length * width

# After refactoring

def calculate_area(length, width=None):

if width is None:

return length * length

else:

return length * width
```

Long Methods

Symptom: Methods contain a large number of lines of code, making them hard to understand.

Solution: Break down long methods into smaller, focused ones. Each method should have a single responsibility, making the code more readable and maintainable. Use meaningful names for the extracted methods to convey their purpose.

```
// Before refactoring
```

```
public void processOrder(Order order) {

// Many lines of code for order processing

}

// After refactoring

public void validateOrder(Order order) {

// Validation logic

}

public void calculateTotal(Order order) {

// Total calculation logic

}

public void updateInventory(Order order) {

// Inventory update logic

}
```

Large Classes

Symptom: Classes have too many responsibilities and methods, violating the Single Responsibility Principle (SRP).

Solution: Refactor large classes into smaller ones, each with a single responsibility. Use composition to combine these smaller classes when necessary. This approach adheres to the SRP and makes the codebase more modular.

```
# Before refactoring

class Order:
```

```python
def __init__(self):
```

 # Many attributes and methods related to order processing

 # After refactoring

```python
class Order:
```

```python
def __init__(self):
```

```python
self.customer = Customer()
```

```python
self.items = []
```

```python
class Customer:
```

```python
def __init__(self):
```

```python
self.name = ""
```

```python
self.email = ""
```

Complex Conditional Logic

Symptom: Code contains deeply nested if statements, complex boolean expressions, or excessive switch/case statements.

Solution: Simplify conditional logic by using techniques like early returns, guard clauses, and extracting complex conditions into descriptive boolean variables or functions. This improves code readability and testability.

// Before refactoring

```javascript
function calculateDiscount(order) {
```

```javascript
if (order.totalAmount > 1000 && order.customerType === 'VIP' && !order.isExpired) {
```

```
// Complex discount calculation logic

}

// More code

}

// After refactoring

function calculateDiscount(order) {

if (isEligibleForDiscount(order)) {

// Simplified discount calculation logic

}

// More code

}

function isEligibleForDiscount(order) {

return order.totalAmount > 1000 && order.customerType ===
'VIP' && !order.isExpired;

}
```

These are just a few examples of common code smells and their solutions. Identifying and addressing code smells can significantly improve code quality and maintainability. Regular code reviews and a focus on clean code principles are essential for maintaining a healthy codebase.

Section 17.3: Heuristic Guidelines for Clean Code

Writing clean code is a subjective art, but there are some heuristic guidelines that can help developers create code that is more maintainable and readable. These guidelines provide practical advice for making code cleaner and adhering to clean code principles. Keep in mind that these are not strict rules but rather recommendations to consider.

1. **Use Meaningful Names**: Choose clear and descriptive names for variables, functions, classes, and other identifiers. A good name should reveal the purpose and intent of the element.

2. **Keep Functions Small**: Follow the Single Responsibility Principle (SRP) by ensuring that functions have a single, well-defined purpose. If a function becomes too long or complex, consider refactoring it into smaller functions.

3. **Minimize Side Effects**: Functions should not have hidden side effects, such as modifying global variables or external state. A function's behavior should be predictable based on its inputs and outputs.

4. **Avoid Deep Nesting**: Reduce code complexity by avoiding excessive nesting of loops and conditional statements. Deeply nested code is harder to understand and test.

5. **Comments Should Explain Why, Not What**: Write comments that explain the why behind a piece of code, not just what it does. Well-written code should be self-explanatory, and comments should provide context or rationale.

6. **Follow Consistent Formatting**: Adhere to consistent code formatting throughout the project. Consistency in formatting helps maintain readability and makes it easier

for developers to work on the codebase.

7. **Test Code Extensively**: Write unit tests to verify the correctness of your code. Testing should be an integral part of the development process, and tests should cover different scenarios and edge cases.

8. **Refactor Regularly**: Don't be afraid to refactor your code when necessary. Refactoring improves code quality and maintainability over time. Use tools and IDE support to help with refactoring.

9. **Think About the Next Developer**: Write code as if the next person who reads it is a psychopath who knows where you live. In other words, prioritize clarity and documentation in your code.

10. **Review and Collaborate**: Conduct code reviews with your peers to get feedback on your code. Collaborative efforts often lead to better code quality.

11. **Keep It Simple**: Simplicity is a virtue. Avoid overengineering and complex solutions when a simpler approach will suffice. Simple code is easier to maintain.

12. **Document When Necessary**: While code should be self-explanatory, there are cases where additional documentation is beneficial, such as API documentation or explaining complex algorithms.

13. **Version Control**: Use version control systems like Git to track changes to your codebase. This allows for easy collaboration, history tracking, and the ability to revert to previous states.

14. **Keep Dependencies in Check**: Limit the number of external dependencies in your project. Excessive dependencies can complicate the build process and introduce compatibility issues.

15. **Learn and Improve**: Continuously learn and improve

your coding skills. Stay updated with best practices and new technologies to become a better developer.

These heuristic guidelines serve as a starting point for writing clean code, but they should be adapted to the specific needs and context of your project. Ultimately, writing clean code is an ongoing process that requires practice, feedback, and a commitment to producing high-quality software.

Section 17.4: Applying Heuristics to Real Projects

Applying heuristics and best practices for writing clean code is essential, but real-world projects often come with unique challenges and trade-offs. In this section, we'll explore how these heuristic guidelines can be applied in practice and adapted to address the complexities of actual software development projects.

1. **Use Case-Specific Naming**: While meaningful names are important, they should also be contextually relevant to the project. In some cases, domain-specific terminology may be necessary to accurately reflect the problem domain.

2. **Balancing Function Size**: Striking a balance between small, focused functions and practicality is crucial. It's not always feasible to keep functions extremely small, especially in complex domains. Prioritize clarity over adhering to an arbitrary size limit.

3. **Managing Side Effects**: Real projects may require interaction with external systems, databases, or APIs, which inherently involve side effects. While minimizing side effects is ideal, it's essential to manage them through proper error handling and encapsulation.

4. **Documenting Complex Algorithms**: In cases where

complex algorithms are necessary, provide comprehensive documentation that explains the algorithm's purpose, steps, and any relevant mathematical or scientific concepts. Use comments and, if needed, external documentation.

5. **Maintaining Consistency**: Consistency in code formatting and style is essential for collaborative projects. Teams should establish and adhere to coding conventions, leveraging tools like linters and code formatters to automate consistency checks.

6. **Test-Driven Development (TDD)**: TDD can be a powerful approach to ensure code correctness. However, it may not be suitable for all projects, especially legacy systems. Evaluate whether TDD is appropriate for your project's goals and constraints.

7. **Refactoring Legacy Code**: Legacy codebases often require extensive refactoring to meet modern standards. Plan refactoring efforts carefully, prioritize high-risk areas, and ensure comprehensive test coverage to maintain functionality.

8. **Clear and Concise Documentation**: Documentation should strike a balance between clarity and brevity. Use documentation tools, such as docstrings and comments, to provide in-code explanations, and maintain external documentation for broader project context.

9. **Version Control and Collaboration**: Effective use of version control is crucial in team projects. Implement branching and merging strategies that suit the project's needs, and ensure team members are well-versed in collaborative practices.

10. **Dependency Management**: Carefully evaluate dependencies and their impact on project maintainability and stability. Consider version compatibility, licensing,

and alternatives when adding external libraries or frameworks.

11. **Simplicity in Design**: Aim for simplicity in architectural design. Complexity should only be introduced when justified by project requirements. Maintain a clear separation of concerns, adhere to design patterns, and refactor as needed to simplify the architecture.

12. **Accessibility and Internationalization**: For projects with diverse user bases, prioritize accessibility and internationalization. Ensure that the codebase is adaptable to various languages and that it complies with accessibility standards.

13. **Scalability and Performance**: As projects grow, scalability and performance become critical concerns. Keep an eye on potential bottlenecks and inefficiencies, and address them through profiling, optimization, and architectural improvements.

14. **Security**: Make security a primary consideration from the outset. Implement secure coding practices, perform code reviews with a focus on security vulnerabilities, and stay informed about emerging threats and solutions.

15. **Continuous Improvement**: Encourage a culture of continuous improvement within your development team. Regularly review and adapt coding practices, learn from past mistakes, and seek opportunities to enhance code quality.

In summary, while heuristic guidelines provide a solid foundation for clean code, flexibility and adaptability are key when applying them to real projects. The ability to balance best practices with project-specific requirements and constraints is crucial for successful software development. Keep learning, experimenting, and refining your approach to consistently produce clean and maintainable code.

Section 17.5: Continuous Improvement

Continuous improvement is a fundamental principle in the world of software development and clean code. It encapsulates the idea that the pursuit of excellence is an ongoing process. In this section, we'll delve into the importance of continuous improvement and how it applies to writing clean and maintainable code.

1. **Iterative Refinement**: Clean code is not achieved in a single leap but through an iterative process. Teams should routinely review and refactor code to enhance its quality. This process of refining code incrementally is essential for long-term maintainability.

2. **Code Reviews**: Regular code reviews provide an opportunity for team members to share knowledge, identify issues, and collectively make improvements. They serve as a quality control mechanism and foster a culture of learning.

3. **Learn from Mistakes**: Mistakes are a natural part of software development. What's crucial is learning from them. When issues arise, conduct post-mortems or retrospectives to understand the root causes and implement preventive measures.

4. **Coding Standards Evolution**: Coding standards should evolve alongside changing project requirements and industry best practices. Regularly revisit and update coding standards to align with the team's current needs.

5. **Knowledge Sharing**: Encourage knowledge sharing within the team. Conduct internal workshops, brown bag sessions, or knowledge transfer meetings to disseminate

best practices, new tools, and techniques.

6. **Mentoring**: Experienced team members should mentor junior developers. This mentorship helps junior developers learn clean coding principles faster and reinforces good habits.

7. **Refactor with Confidence**: Maintain a comprehensive suite of unit tests to refactor code with confidence. Automated tests act as a safety net, ensuring that changes do not introduce regressions.

8. **Tooling and Automation**: Leverage automated tools for code analysis, formatting, and testing. These tools help maintain consistency and reduce manual effort.

9. **Community Involvement**: Encourage developers to participate in the broader developer community. Engaging in open-source projects, attending conferences, and contributing to forums can expose team members to new ideas and best practices.

10. **Feedback Loops**: Establish feedback loops with stakeholders, such as product owners and end-users. Gather feedback on the usability and functionality of the software, and use this input to inform future development efforts.

11. **Agile Practices**: Adopt agile development practices like Scrum or Kanban, which emphasize regular retrospectives to identify areas for improvement and adapt to changing requirements.

12. **Documentation and Knowledge Base**: Maintain an up-to-date knowledge base and documentation repository. Well-organized documentation aids in onboarding new team members and serves as a reference for best practices.

13. **Technical Debt Management**: Keep an eye on accumulating technical debt. Plan and allocate time for

addressing technical debt as part of regular development sprints.

14. **Measurement and Metrics**: Use metrics to track code quality, project progress, and team performance. Metrics can provide valuable insights into areas that require attention.

15. **Psychological Safety**: Foster a culture of psychological safety, where team members feel comfortable sharing ideas, concerns, and failures without fear of blame. This openness promotes learning and improvement.

16. **Innovation**: Encourage innovation and experimentation. Allocate time for exploring new technologies and approaches that could benefit the project.

17. **Retrospective Meetings**: Regularly hold retrospective meetings to reflect on recent development cycles. Discuss what went well, what didn't, and what can be improved in the next iteration.

18. **Celebrate Successes**: Celebrate achievements and milestones, whether they are related to code quality, project completion, or team growth. Recognize and reward excellence.

In conclusion, the pursuit of clean code and software craftsmanship is a continuous journey. It requires commitment, a growth mindset, and a willingness to adapt. By embracing the principles of continuous improvement, development teams can consistently produce high-quality code that meets the evolving needs of their projects and organizations.

Section 18.1: More on Concurrency Challenges

Concurrency is a critical aspect of modern software development, and it often comes with a set of complex challenges. In this section, we will delve deeper into some of the advanced concurrency challenges that developers may encounter when building concurrent systems.

1. **Deadlocks**: Deadlocks occur when two or more threads are unable to proceed because each is waiting for the other to release a resource. Detecting and resolving deadlocks is a non-trivial task, and various strategies, such as using timeouts and deadlock detection algorithms, can be employed to mitigate this issue.

2. **Starvation**: Starvation happens when a thread or process is continually denied access to a resource it needs. This can occur in scenarios where certain threads are given higher priority, causing others to be starved. Proper thread scheduling algorithms and fairness mechanisms must be in place to prevent this.

3. **Livelocks**: Livelocks are similar to deadlocks but involve threads repeatedly changing their state in response to the actions of others, without making progress. Identifying and mitigating livelocks can be challenging due to their dynamic nature.

4. **Thread-Safety Challenges**: Ensuring thread safety in concurrent systems requires careful consideration. Even seemingly simple operations can lead to race conditions or data corruption if not properly synchronized. Developers need to use synchronization primitives like locks, semaphores, and monitors effectively.

5. **Efficiency and Scalability**: Designing concurrent systems

that efficiently utilize hardware resources and scale well with increasing workloads can be a complex task. Strategies such as fine-grained locking, lock-free data structures, and load balancing are essential for achieving high performance.

6. **Resource Management**: Effective management of resources like memory, file handles, and network connections in a concurrent environment is crucial to prevent resource leaks and system instability. Developers must be mindful of acquiring and releasing resources correctly.

7. **Testing and Debugging**: Debugging concurrent code can be challenging due to the non-deterministic nature of race conditions and concurrency-related bugs. Proper testing techniques, including stress testing and the use of tools like thread analyzers, are essential to identify and fix issues.

8. **Fault Tolerance**: In distributed and concurrent systems, components can fail independently. Designing for fault tolerance, where the system can continue to operate despite failures, is a complex challenge that involves redundancy, error detection, and recovery mechanisms.

9. **Complex Data Sharing**: Concurrent systems often involve sharing data among multiple threads or processes. Managing this shared data, ensuring data consistency, and preventing data races require careful design and synchronization techniques.

10. **Ordering and Synchronization**: Establishing a consistent order of execution among threads is crucial for correctness. Techniques like barriers, atomic operations, and memory ordering semantics are used to ensure proper synchronization.

11. **Thread Pools and Work Distribution**: Designing efficient

thread pools and work distribution mechanisms is essential for parallelism. Load balancing algorithms and work-stealing techniques can help maximize CPU utilization.

12. **Real-time and Low-Latency Requirements**: Some applications, such as real-time systems or financial trading platforms, have strict latency requirements. Meeting these demands while ensuring correctness adds an extra layer of complexity to concurrency design.

13. **Hardware-Specific Challenges**: Different hardware architectures and operating systems may have unique concurrency challenges and optimizations. Understanding the underlying platform is crucial for optimizing performance.

14. **Testing for Race Conditions**: Testing tools and techniques like race condition detectors and model checking tools can help identify and eliminate race conditions during development and testing phases.

15. **Concurrency Models**: Different concurrency models, such as actor-based concurrency or dataflow programming, provide alternative approaches to managing concurrency challenges. Choosing the right model for a specific application is an important decision.

In conclusion, mastering concurrency is a vital skill for modern software developers, but it comes with a range of advanced challenges. Addressing these challenges requires a deep understanding of concurrent programming principles, synchronization mechanisms, and the specific requirements of the application being developed. By tackling these issues effectively, developers can build robust and high-performance concurrent systems.

Section 18.2: Advanced Concurrency Patterns

Concurrency is a powerful tool for building efficient and responsive software, but it also introduces complexity. Advanced concurrency patterns provide higher-level abstractions and solutions to common challenges in concurrent programming. In this section, we will explore some of these patterns and how they can be applied.

1. Producer-Consumer Pattern

The producer-consumer pattern is a classic concurrency pattern where one or more producer threads generate data, and one or more consumer threads consume that data. A shared data structure, often a queue, is used to pass data between producers and consumers. This pattern is useful for scenarios like task scheduling, message passing, and parallel data processing.

```java
import java.util.concurrent.BlockingQueue;

import java.util.concurrent.LinkedBlockingQueue;

class Producer implements Runnable {

private final BlockingQueue<Integer> queue;

public Producer(BlockingQueue<Integer> queue) {

this.queue = queue;

}

@Override

public void run() {

try {
```

```java
for (int i = 0; i < 10; i++) {

queue.put(i);

System.out.println("Produced: " + i);

Thread.sleep(100);

}

} catch (InterruptedException e) {

Thread.currentThread().interrupt();

}

}

}

class Consumer implements Runnable {

private final BlockingQueue<Integer> queue;

public Consumer(BlockingQueue<Integer> queue) {

this.queue = queue;

}

@Override

public void run() {

try {

while (true) {

int value = queue.take();
```

```java
System.out.println("Consumed: " + value);

Thread.sleep(200);

}

} catch (InterruptedException e) {

Thread.currentThread().interrupt();

}

}

}

public class Main {

public static void main(String[] args) {

BlockingQueue<Integer> queue = new LinkedBlockingQueue<>(5);

Thread producerThread = new Thread(new Producer(queue));

Thread consumerThread = new Thread(new Consumer(queue));

producerThread.start();

consumerThread.start();

}

}
```

2. Readers-Writers Pattern

The readers-writers pattern deals with scenarios where multiple threads need to access a shared resource, but some threads only read while others write. It ensures that multiple readers can access the resource simultaneously, but exclusive access is granted to a single writer at a time. This pattern helps balance data access efficiency and consistency.

3. Thread Pool Pattern

A thread pool pattern involves creating a fixed number of worker threads that can execute tasks concurrently. Threads in the pool are reused to execute multiple tasks, reducing the overhead of thread creation and destruction. Thread pools are beneficial in scenarios with a high number of short-lived tasks, such as web servers and application servers.

```java
import java.util.concurrent.ExecutorService;

import java.util.concurrent.Executors;

public class ThreadPoolExample {

public static void main(String[] args) {

// Create a fixed-size thread pool with 4 threads

ExecutorService executor = Executors.newFixedThreadPool(4);

// Submit tasks to the thread pool

for (int i = 0; i < 10; i++) {

final int taskNumber = i;

executor.submit(() -> {

System.out.println("Task " + taskNumber + " executed by " + Thread.currentThread().getName());
```

```
});

}
```

// Shutdown the thread pool when done

```
executor.shutdown();

}

}
```

4. Futures and Promises

Futures and promises provide a way to represent and retrieve the result of an asynchronous operation. A future represents a value that may not be available yet, and a promise is used to set the value of that future once it becomes available. These abstractions are helpful in concurrent programming when dealing with asynchronous tasks and parallelism.

import java.util.concurrent.CompletableFuture;

public class CompletableFutureExample {

public static void main(String[] args) {

// Create a CompletableFuture for an asynchronous task

```
CompletableFuture<Integer>                    future          =
CompletableFuture.supplyAsync(() -> {
```

// Simulate a time-consuming task

try {

```
Thread.sleep(1000);
```

```
} catch (InterruptedException e) {

Thread.currentThread().interrupt();

}

return 42;

});

// Attach a callback to handle the result when it's ready

future.thenAccept(result -> System.out.println("Result: " + result));

// Block until the future completes (not recommended in practice)

future.join();

}

}
```

These are just a few examples of advanced concurrency patterns and techniques that can be applied to solve specific problems in concurrent programming. Depending on your application's requirements, choosing the right pattern can significantly improve code maintainability, scalability, and performance while managing the inherent complexity of concurrent systems.

Section 18.3: Parallelism and Multithreading

Parallelism and multithreading are two fundamental concepts in concurrent programming that enable the execution of tasks simultaneously to improve performance and responsiveness in software systems. In this section, we will explore these concepts and understand their significance.

Parallelism vs. Multithreading

Parallelism refers to the concurrent execution of multiple tasks at the same time, with the goal of improving overall throughput or reducing the time it takes to complete a set of tasks. It is often used in scenarios where tasks are independent and can be executed simultaneously without affecting each other. Parallelism can be achieved through various means, including multicore processors, distributed computing, and specialized hardware accelerators.

Multithreading, on the other hand, is a specific form of parallelism that involves the use of multiple threads within a single process or application. Threads are lightweight units of execution that share the same memory space but have their own execution context, including registers, program counter, and stack. Multithreading is commonly used in applications to perform tasks concurrently, such as handling user interfaces, processing data in the background, or managing network connections.

Benefits of Parallelism and Multithreading

1. **Improved Performance**: By dividing tasks into smaller units that can be executed concurrently, parallelism and multithreading can significantly improve the performance of applications, especially on modern multicore processors.
2. **Responsiveness**: Multithreading allows applications to remain responsive to user input, ensuring that time-consuming tasks do not block the user interface. For example, a web browser can use separate threads to load web pages while keeping the UI responsive.
3. **Efficient Resource Utilization**: Multithreaded applications can efficiently utilize available resources, such as CPU cores, memory, and I/O devices, leading to better

resource management.

Challenges in Parallelism and Multithreading

While parallelism and multithreading offer many benefits, they also introduce challenges and complexities:

1. **Concurrency Issues**: Multithreaded programs may encounter issues like race conditions, deadlocks, and data corruption when multiple threads access shared data concurrently. Proper synchronization mechanisms, like locks and semaphores, are required to address these problems.
2. **Debugging and Testing**: Debugging multithreaded applications can be challenging due to non-deterministic behavior and timing-dependent issues. Thorough testing and the use of debugging tools are essential.
3. **Complexity**: Managing multiple threads, their synchronization, and communication can make the code more complex and harder to maintain. Careful design and adherence to best practices are necessary to mitigate this complexity.

Example: Multithreading in Java

Java provides built-in support for multithreading through its java.lang.Thread class. Here's a simple Java example demonstrating multithreading:

```java
class MyThread extends Thread {

public void run() {

for (int i = 1; i <= 5; i++) {
```

```java
System.out.println("Thread " + Thread.currentThread().getId() + ": "
+ i);

try {

Thread.sleep(1000);

} catch (InterruptedException e) {

Thread.currentThread().interrupt();

}

}

}

}

public class MultithreadingExample {

public static void main(String[] args) {

MyThread thread1 = new MyThread();

MyThread thread2 = new MyThread();

thread1.start();

thread2.start();

}

}
```

In this example, two threads (thread1 and thread2) are created and executed concurrently, printing numbers from 1 to 5 with a one-second delay between each print.

In conclusion, parallelism and multithreading are essential techniques for improving the performance and responsiveness of software systems. However, they also introduce challenges related to concurrency and complexity that developers must address effectively to build robust multithreaded applications.

Section 18.4: Handling Deadlocks and Starvation

Deadlocks and starvation are common issues that can occur in multithreaded programs. In this section, we will discuss these problems, their causes, and strategies to handle them effectively.

Deadlocks

A **deadlock** occurs when two or more threads are unable to proceed because each is waiting for the other to release a resource. In other words, they are stuck in a circular waiting pattern. Deadlocks can lead to a complete halt of the application, causing it to become unresponsive.

Causes of Deadlocks

Deadlocks typically happen due to four necessary conditions:

1. **Mutual Exclusion**: Threads must contend for exclusive access to resources. Only one thread can access a resource at a time.
2. **Hold and Wait**: Threads must hold at least one resource and wait for additional resources that are held by other threads.
3. **No Preemption**: Resources cannot be forcibly taken away from a thread. They can only be released voluntarily.

4. **Circular Wait**: A circular chain of two or more threads exists, where each thread is waiting for a resource held by the next thread in the chain.

Preventing Deadlocks

To prevent deadlocks, you can use several strategies:

- **Lock Ordering**: Establish a global order for acquiring locks and ensure that all threads follow the same order. This can prevent circular waits.

- **Timeouts**: Implement a timeout mechanism where a thread releases resources it holds after a certain period if it cannot acquire all required resources.

- **Resource Allocation Graphs**: Use resource allocation graphs to detect and resolve deadlocks. If the graph contains a cycle, a deadlock is present.

Starvation

Starvation occurs when a thread is unable to gain access to a resource it needs, even though it is eligible to do so. Starved threads may never make progress, leading to unfair resource allocation.

Causes of Starvation

Starvation can happen due to various reasons:

- **Priority Inversion**: Lower-priority threads may preempt higher-priority threads, causing them to starve.

- **Resource Contention**: High contention for resources can lead to some threads repeatedly losing the competition for those resources.

Preventing Starvation

To prevent starvation, you can use techniques like:

- **Priority Scheduling**: Implement priority-based scheduling algorithms to ensure that higher-priority threads are not starved by lower-priority threads.

- **Fair Queuing**: Use fair queuing algorithms that distribute resources more equitably among competing threads.

- **Aging**: Implement aging mechanisms that gradually increase the priority of threads that have been waiting for a long time.

Example: Deadlock Prevention in Java

Here's a simple Java example demonstrating deadlock prevention using lock ordering:

```java
import java.util.concurrent.locks.Lock;

import java.util.concurrent.locks.ReentrantLock;

public class DeadlockPreventionExample {

private static final Lock lock1 = new ReentrantLock();

private static final Lock lock2 = new ReentrantLock();

public static void main(String[] args) {
```

```java
Thread thread1 = new Thread(() -> {

lock1.lock();

try {

Thread.sleep(100);

lock2.lock();

// Perform operations

} catch (InterruptedException e) {

Thread.currentThread().interrupt();

} finally {

lock2.unlock();

lock1.unlock();

}

});

Thread thread2 = new Thread(() -> {

lock1.lock();

try {

lock2.lock();

// Perform operations

} finally {

lock2.unlock();
```

```
lock1.unlock();

}

});

thread1.start();

thread2.start();

}

}
```

In this example, we use lock ordering to ensure that both threads acquire locks in the same order, preventing a circular wait condition.

In conclusion, deadlocks and starvation are important issues to consider when working with multithreaded programs. Preventing and mitigating these problems requires careful design, use of appropriate synchronization mechanisms, and strategies such as lock ordering, timeouts, and priority scheduling.

Section 18.5: Practical Tips for Concurrent Systems

When developing concurrent systems, it's essential to follow best practices to ensure that your application is robust, efficient, and free from common concurrency issues. In this section, we'll provide practical tips for building and maintaining concurrent systems.

1. Understand the Problem Domain

Before diving into concurrent programming, thoroughly understand the problem domain. Identify critical sections, potential resource contention, and dependencies. A clear understanding of the problem will help you make informed decisions about concurrency strategies.

2. Use Thread-Safe Data Structures

Whenever possible, use thread-safe data structures provided by your programming language or libraries. These data structures are designed to handle concurrent access safely, reducing the likelihood of race conditions.

3. Minimize Shared State

Shared state is a common source of concurrency issues. Minimize shared state by using immutable objects and avoiding global variables. When shared state is necessary, use synchronization mechanisms like locks to protect access.

4. Favor High-Level Concurrency Abstractions

Modern programming languages and libraries offer high-level concurrency abstractions like futures, promises, and actors. These abstractions simplify concurrent programming and reduce the risk of low-level mistakes.

5. Follow the Principle of Least Privilege

When granting access to shared resources, follow the principle of least privilege. Only provide the necessary access permissions to minimize the potential for unintended consequences.

6. Embrace Asynchronous Programming

Asynchronous programming can improve the scalability and responsiveness of your application. Use asynchronous techniques, such as callbacks, promises, or async/await, to handle concurrency when appropriate.

7. Profile and Monitor

Regularly profile and monitor your concurrent application to identify performance bottlenecks, contention issues, and potential deadlocks. Tools and profilers can help you pinpoint problems and optimize your code.

8. Test Thoroughly

Concurrent code is notoriously challenging to test. Implement comprehensive unit tests, integration tests, and stress tests to validate the correctness and performance of your concurrent components.

9. Use Proper Synchronization

When using locks or other synchronization mechanisms, be mindful of potential deadlocks. Always release locks in the reverse order they were acquired to avoid circular waits.

10. Graceful Shutdown

Implement graceful shutdown procedures for your concurrent systems. Ensure that all resources are released, and threads are properly terminated when the application exits or undergoes maintenance.

11. Plan for Scalability

Consider the scalability of your concurrent system. Design your application to handle increasing loads gracefully by using techniques like load balancing and sharding.

12. Document Concurrency Strategies

Document your concurrency strategies, especially if your code uses complex synchronization mechanisms. Clear documentation helps other developers understand the rationale and usage of concurrency-related constructs.

13. Stay Informed

Concurrency programming is a rapidly evolving field. Stay informed about the latest developments, best practices, and tools related to concurrent programming to keep your skills up-to-date.

In conclusion, building concurrent systems requires careful planning, attention to detail, and adherence to best practices. By understanding the problem domain, using appropriate abstractions, minimizing shared state, and following these practical tips, you can develop robust and efficient concurrent applications while avoiding common pitfalls.

Chapter 19: Appendix B: Decimal I/O

Section 19.1: Decimal Formatting and Parsing

In this section, we'll explore decimal formatting and parsing, an essential aspect of software development that deals with converting numerical data to and from human-readable strings. Properly formatting and parsing decimal numbers is crucial for applications that work with financial data, scientific calculations, or any domain involving precise numeric representation.

Decimal Number Representation

Decimal numbers, also known as floating-point numbers, are a common way to represent real numbers with fractional parts in computing. These numbers are typically stored in a binary format, which can lead to challenges when displaying or parsing them as human-readable strings.

For example, the decimal number 1/10, which is 0.1 in decimal notation, cannot be precisely represented in binary. This can result in inaccuracies when working with decimal numbers in binary form.

Formatting Decimal Numbers

Formatting decimal numbers involves converting a numeric value into a string with a specific format, such as currency formatting or scientific notation. Proper formatting ensures that the number is presented in a way that is understandable and meaningful to users.

Here's an example of formatting a decimal number in Python:

amount = 1234.5678

formatted_amount = "{:.2f}".format(amount)

print(formatted_amount) # *Output: "1234.57"*

In this example, the "{:.2f}" format specifier is used to format the amount with two decimal places.

Parsing Decimal Numbers

Parsing, on the other hand, involves converting a string containing a decimal number back into a numeric data type that can be used in calculations. Proper parsing ensures that the string is correctly interpreted, and any formatting or locale-specific issues are handled appropriately.

Here's an example of parsing a formatted decimal number in Python:

formatted_amount = "1234.57"

parsed_amount = float(formatted_amount)

print(parsed_amount) # *Output: 1234.57*

In this example, the float() function is used to parse the formatted_amount string and convert it back to a floating-point number.

Challenges in Decimal I/O

Decimal I/O can be challenging due to several factors:

1. **Precision and Rounding**: When converting between decimal and binary representations, precision and rounding issues can occur. For example, rounding errors can accumulate in financial applications.
2. **Locale and Culture**: Different locales and cultures have

varying conventions for decimal separators, thousands separators, and numeric formats. It's essential to consider these differences when formatting and parsing decimal numbers.

3. **Handling Errors**: When parsing user input or data from external sources, error handling is critical. You need to handle cases where the input is not a valid decimal number.
4. **Performance**: Depending on the programming language and libraries used, parsing and formatting decimal numbers can have performance implications, especially when dealing with large datasets.

In this appendix, we will delve into the details of decimal formatting and parsing, explore common challenges, and provide guidelines and best practices for handling decimal I/O effectively in your applications.

Section 19.2: Challenges in Decimal I/O

While decimal formatting and parsing are fundamental tasks in software development, they come with a set of challenges that developers need to address. In this section, we'll explore some of the common challenges associated with decimal I/O and discuss strategies to overcome them.

1. Precision and Rounding

One of the most significant challenges in decimal I/O is dealing with precision and rounding errors. Decimal numbers are often stored in binary format, leading to discrepancies when converting them to and from their string representations.

Consider the following Python example:

amount = 0.1 + 0.1 + 0.1 *# Represents 0.3 in decimal*

formatted_amount = "{:.1f}".format(amount)

print(formatted_amount) *# Output: "0.3"*

While you might expect the output to be "0.3," the binary representation of these fractions introduces rounding errors. Such issues can be critical in financial applications where exact precision is required.

To address precision challenges, developers often use specialized libraries or data types for decimal arithmetic that provide higher accuracy, such as Python's decimal module.

2. Locale and Culture Differences

Decimal formatting and parsing can be affected by locale and culture differences. Different regions and languages have their own conventions for decimal separators (e.g., "." or ","), thousands separators (e.g., "," or "."), and numeric formats.

To handle locale-specific formatting, developers should consider using libraries or functions that allow customization based on the user's locale settings. This ensures that decimal numbers are presented in a format familiar to the user.

3. Handling Errors

When parsing user input or data from external sources, it's crucial to implement robust error handling for decimal I/O. Users may provide invalid or improperly formatted input, which can lead to runtime errors if not handled correctly.

For example, consider parsing a user-entered string in Python:

```python
user_input = "abc"

try:

parsed_value = float(user_input)

except ValueError as e:

print(f"Error: {e}")
```

In this case, attempting to parse the string "abc" as a float will raise a ValueError. To prevent crashes, developers should include appropriate error handling and validation mechanisms when dealing with user input.

4. Performance Considerations

The performance of decimal I/O operations can vary depending on the programming language, libraries, and data volume. Parsing and formatting decimal numbers can be computationally expensive, especially when dealing with large datasets or frequent conversions.

Developers should profile their applications and consider optimization techniques such as caching parsed values or using efficient parsing libraries if performance is a concern.

In summary, working with decimal I/O involves addressing challenges related to precision, locale differences, error handling, and performance. These challenges require careful consideration and the use of appropriate tools and techniques to ensure accurate and efficient decimal operations in software applications.

Section 19.3: Writing a Decimal Formatter

When dealing with decimal I/O, one common task is formatting decimal numbers into strings. In this section, we'll explore the process of writing a decimal formatter—a component responsible for converting decimal values into human-readable strings. While many programming languages provide built-in functions or libraries for this purpose, understanding the fundamentals of writing a custom decimal formatter can be valuable for specialized formatting needs or learning purposes.

Basic Decimal Formatting

Let's begin with a simple example in Python, where we'll write a basic decimal formatter function. This function takes a decimal number and returns its string representation with a specified number of decimal places.

```python
def format_decimal(number, decimal_places=2):

return f"{number:.{decimal_places}f}"
```

Here, we use Python's f-strings and the .format() specifier to control the number of decimal places. You can use this function as follows:

```python
amount = 123.456789

formatted_amount = format_decimal(amount, decimal_places=2)

print(formatted_amount) # Output: "123.46"
```

This basic formatter works well for simple cases, but real-world scenarios often involve more complex formatting requirements.

Handling Locale-Specific Formatting

In applications that target international audiences, it's crucial to support locale-specific formatting. Different regions may use different decimal separators (e.g., "." or ","), thousands separators (e.g., "," or "."), and numeric formats.

To handle locale-specific formatting, you can use libraries or functions that allow customization based on the user's locale settings. For instance, in Python, the locale module can be used to format numbers according to the user's locale:

```python
import locale

def format_decimal_locale(number, locale_name="en_US.UTF-8"):

locale.setlocale(locale.LC_ALL, locale_name)

return locale.format_string("%.2f", number)
```

In this example, we use the locale module to set the locale and then format the number accordingly:

```python
amount = 1234567.89

formatted_amount = format_decimal_locale(amount, locale_name="fr_FR.UTF-8")

print(formatted_amount) # Output: "1 234 567,89"
```

Customizing Formatting

In many applications, you might need to customize decimal formatting further. This could involve adding currency symbols, specifying whether negative numbers should be enclosed in parentheses, or handling special cases.

For example, here's a Python function that formats a number as currency:

```python
def format_currency(number, currency_symbol="$"):

return f"{currency_symbol}{number:.2f}"
```

You can use this function to format currency values with a specified currency symbol:

amount = 1234.56

formatted_amount   =   format_currency(amount, currency_symbol="€")

print(formatted_amount) # *Output: "€1234.56"*

Decimal Formatting Libraries

While writing custom decimal formatters can be educational, it's often more practical to use specialized libraries for complex formatting needs. Many programming languages provide libraries like DecimalFormat in Java, NumberFormat in JavaScript, and Intl.NumberFormat in ECMAScript, which offer extensive options for decimal formatting based on locale, currency, and more.

In summary, writing a decimal formatter involves creating a function or component that converts decimal numbers into formatted strings. Depending on your application's requirements, you may need to consider locale-specific formatting, customize formatting rules, and use specialized libraries to simplify complex formatting tasks.

Section 19.4: Designing the Decimal Parser

In the previous section, we discussed formatting decimal numbers into strings. Now, let's dive into the reverse process—parsing formatted decimal strings into numeric values. Parsing is a fundamental operation when dealing with user input, file processing, or data interchange between systems. Designing an efficient and robust decimal parser is essential for handling diverse input formats and ensuring data integrity.

Challenges in Decimal Parsing

Decimal parsing can be challenging due to several factors:

1. **Locale Variations:** Different locales use various symbols and conventions for decimal points, thousands separators, and numeric representations. For instance, in some locales, a comma (",") is used as the decimal separator, while others use a period ("."). Handling these variations is crucial for internationalization.

2. **Number Formats:** Numbers can be represented in various formats, including scientific notation (e.g., "1.23e4"), percent notation (e.g., "12.34%"), and currency notation (e.g., "$1,234.56"). A robust parser should recognize and handle these formats.

3. **User Errors:** Users may input numbers with typos, missing separators, or incorrect formats. The parser should gracefully handle such errors and provide meaningful feedback.

Basic Decimal Parsing

Let's start with a basic decimal parser example in Python. This parser takes a string and attempts to convert it into a numeric value:

```python
def parse_decimal(text):

try:

return float(text)

except ValueError:

raise ValueError("Invalid decimal format")
```

This simple parser uses Python's float() function, which can handle various numeric formats. If the input is not a valid number, it raises a ValueError.

```python
input_text = "123.45"

parsed_value = parse_decimal(input_text)

print(parsed_value) # Output: 123.45
```

Handling Locale-Specific Parsing

To handle locale-specific parsing, you can use libraries or functions that consider the user's locale settings. Python's locale module can be used in conjunction with a custom parser to handle locale-specific formats:

```python
import locale

def parse_decimal_locale(text, locale_name="en_US.UTF-8"):

locale.setlocale(locale.LC_ALL, locale_name)

try:

return locale.atof(text)

except ValueError:

raise ValueError("Invalid decimal format")
```

In this example, we set the locale using locale.setlocale() and then use locale.atof() to parse the text. The locale settings ensure that the parser correctly recognizes the decimal separator and thousands separator for the specified locale.

```python
input_text = "1,234.56"
```

parsed_value = parse_decimal_locale(input_text, locale_name="fr_FR.UTF-8")

print(parsed_value) # *Output: 1234.56*

Customizing Parsing

Depending on your application's requirements, you may need to customize the parsing process. For instance, you might want to support parsing of numbers with currency symbols, units of measure, or specific numeric conventions. Customization often involves writing a more complex parser that can recognize and extract relevant information from the input text.

In summary, designing a decimal parser involves creating a component that can convert formatted decimal strings into numeric values. Challenges include handling locale variations, recognizing diverse number formats, and gracefully handling user input errors. While basic parsing can be done with built-in functions, custom parsers may be needed for more specialized requirements.

Section 19.5: Error Handling in Decimal I/O

When working with decimal formatting and parsing, error handling is a critical aspect of ensuring data integrity and providing a good user experience. In this section, we'll explore various error scenarios that can occur during decimal input and output operations and discuss best practices for handling them.

Common Error Scenarios

1. **Invalid Format:** Users may input data in an incorrect format, such as missing decimal points, thousands separators, or using unsupported characters. Handling

these errors gracefully is essential to prevent data corruption.

2. **Locale Mismatch:** In international applications, users from different locales may have varying conventions for decimal separators and thousands separators. Failing to account for locale differences can lead to parsing errors.

3. **Overflow and Precision Loss:** Decimal numbers can become very large or have high precision. If the input exceeds the system's limits, it may result in overflow or precision loss, affecting the accuracy of calculations.

Handling Errors in Decimal Formatting

When formatting decimal numbers into strings, it's crucial to check for errors and handle them appropriately. Here's an example in Python that demonstrates error handling during decimal formatting:

```python
def format_decimal(number, locale_name="en_US.UTF-8"):

try:

import locale

locale.setlocale(locale.LC_ALL, locale_name)

return locale.format_string("%.2f", number)

except (ValueError, locale.Error):

raise ValueError("Invalid number or locale")
```

In this example, we use Python's locale module to format the number as a string. If any errors occur during formatting, such as an invalid number or locale, we raise a ValueError with an error message.

Handling Errors in Decimal Parsing

Error handling during decimal parsing is equally important. When users input numbers, they may make mistakes, and it's the application's responsibility to provide feedback and prevent incorrect data from being processed. Here's a Python example of error handling during decimal parsing:

```python
def parse_decimal(text, locale_name="en_US.UTF-8"):

try:

import locale

locale.setlocale(locale.LC_ALL, locale_name)

return locale.atof(text)

except (ValueError, locale.Error):

raise ValueError("Invalid decimal format")
```

In this parser, we attempt to parse the input text into a numeric value using the locale.atof() function. If any errors occur, such as an invalid format or locale, we raise a ValueError with a descriptive error message.

Providing User-Friendly Feedback

When handling errors in decimal I/O, it's essential to provide user-friendly feedback. This includes clear error messages that explain what went wrong and how the user can correct it. Additionally, consider providing suggestions or auto-correction options when possible.

For example, if a user enters "1.23a" instead of "1.23," the error message could suggest, "Invalid character 'a.' Please enter a valid decimal number."

Logging and Monitoring

In production systems, logging and monitoring are crucial for identifying and diagnosing errors. You can use logging frameworks like Python's logging module to record errors and exceptions. Monitoring tools can help you track error rates and patterns, allowing you to proactively address issues.

In conclusion, error handling is an essential aspect of working with decimal I/O operations. By carefully considering and handling common error scenarios during formatting and parsing, you can ensure data integrity, improve user experience, and maintain the reliability of your software. Providing clear feedback to users and implementing logging and monitoring mechanisms are key practices for robust error handling.

Chapter 20: Appendix C: How to Transform Employee

Section 20.1: Refactoring Employee's Design

In this section, we'll dive into the process of refactoring the design of an Employee class. Refactoring is the practice of improving code by making small, incremental changes without altering its external behavior. It's an essential skill for maintaining clean code and ensuring that software remains adaptable as requirements evolve.

Analyzing the Existing Design

Before we start refactoring, it's crucial to understand the problems with the existing design of the Employee class. Common issues might include:

1. **Large and Complex Class:** The class may be large and handle too many responsibilities, violating the Single Responsibility Principle (SRP).
2. **Tight Coupling:** High coupling with other classes or dependencies can make the code less flexible and harder to test.
3. **Lack of Abstraction:** The class might not have proper abstractions, making it challenging to extend or modify.
4. **Inadequate Testability:** Poorly designed classes can be challenging to unit test in isolation.
5. **Violation of Open-Closed Principle (OCP):** The class may not be open for extension but closed for modification, making it difficult to add new functionality.

Restructuring the Class

To transform the Employee class, we'll follow these steps:

1. **Identify Responsibilities:** Determine the distinct responsibilities that the Employee class should have. For example, it might be responsible for storing employee information and calculating bonuses.
2. **Extract Classes:** Create new classes for each responsibility identified in the previous step. For instance, you might create an EmployeeInformation class to manage employee data and a BonusCalculator class to handle bonus calculations.
3. **Dependency Injection:** Use dependency injection to provide dependencies, such as database connections or configuration settings, to the new classes.
4. **Encapsulation:** Ensure that each class encapsulates its data and behavior appropriately.
5. **Testing:** Write unit tests for the new classes to verify their functionality. Proper testing is crucial to ensure that refactoring doesn't introduce regressions.
6. **Integration:** Integrate the new classes into the existing system gradually. Replace usages of the old Employee class with the new classes.
7. **Clean Up:** Remove any redundant code from the old Employee class and simplify it as much as possible.

Benefits of Refactoring

Refactoring the Employee class offers several benefits:

- **Improved Maintainability:** The code becomes more modular and easier to maintain, as each class has a single responsibility.

- **Enhanced Testability:** The new classes can be unit-tested in isolation, leading to more reliable software.

- **Flexibility:** The code becomes more adaptable to future changes, adhering to the Open-Closed Principle.

- **Clarity:** The intent of each class is clear, making the codebase more understandable.

- **Reduced Risk:** Refactoring reduces the risk of introducing bugs when adding new features or fixing issues.

Conclusion

Refactoring is an ongoing process that contributes to clean code and maintainable software. By analyzing and restructuring the Employee class, you've taken a step towards improving the overall design of your software. Remember that refactoring should be performed incrementally and with proper testing to ensure the stability of your application.

Section 20.2: Analyzing and Identifying Problems

In this section, we will continue our journey of transforming the Employee class by analyzing the existing problems in its design. Identifying these issues is a crucial first step in the refactoring process.

Bloated Class

One of the primary problems with the current Employee class is that it's likely bloated with various responsibilities. This goes against the Single Responsibility Principle (SRP), which states that a class should have only one reason to change. In our case, the Employee class might be responsible for both managing employee information and calculating bonuses.

Lack of Abstraction

A well-designed class should provide a clear abstraction that hides its implementation details. The current Employee class may expose internal data members and methods that should be hidden. This lack of abstraction makes it challenging to extend or modify the class without affecting its clients.

Coupling

High coupling between classes can lead to several issues, including reduced maintainability and testability. The Employee class might be tightly coupled with other parts of the system, making it less flexible and harder to test in isolation.

Testability

Effective testing is a cornerstone of clean code. However, the current design of the Employee class might hinder testability. If it's challenging to create unit tests for the class without setting up complex dependencies or dealing with excessive setup, it's a sign that the design needs improvement.

Open-Closed Principle Violation

The Open-Closed Principle (OCP) suggests that software entities should be open for extension but closed for modification. In other words, we should be able to add new functionality without changing existing code. The current Employee class might violate this principle, making it difficult to introduce new features without altering the class itself.

Inadequate Separation of Concerns

Clean code emphasizes the separation of concerns, where different aspects of a system are handled by distinct modules or classes. The Employee class may mix concerns, such as data storage and bonus calculation, which should ideally be separated for better code organization.

In the next sections, we'll address these issues one by one as we refactor the Employee class, aiming to create a more maintainable, testable, and extensible design while adhering to clean code principles.

Section 20.3: Restructuring Employee's Class

In this section, we'll delve into the process of restructuring the Employee class to address the identified problems and adhere to clean code principles. We'll work through a series of steps to transform the class into a more maintainable and extensible design.

Step 1: Identify Responsibilities

To adhere to the Single Responsibility Principle (SRP), we must identify and separate the responsibilities within the Employee class. We can begin by identifying the primary responsibilities:

1. **Employee Information:** This includes properties like name, ID, department, and other personal details.
2. **Bonus Calculation:** This involves logic for calculating bonuses based on various criteria.

Step 2: Create Separate Classes

Once we've identified these distinct responsibilities, we can create separate classes for each of them:

EmployeeInfo Class

This class will handle the storage and management of employee information, including properties like name, ID, and department. Here's a simplified example in Python:

```python
class EmployeeInfo:

    def __init__(self, name, employee_id, department):

        self.name = name

        self.employee_id = employee_id

        self.department = department
```

BonusCalculator Class

The BonusCalculator class will encapsulate the logic for calculating bonuses. It can take EmployeeInfo objects as input and compute bonuses based on specific rules.

```python
class BonusCalculator:

    @staticmethod

    def calculate_bonus(employee_info):

        # Logic for bonus calculation based on employee_info

        pass
```

Step 3: Decouple Classes

To minimize coupling, we'll ensure that these classes interact through well-defined interfaces rather than direct dependencies. In this case, BonusCalculator will depend on EmployeeInfo objects, but not the other way around.

Step 4: Unit Testing

With these separate classes, we can easily write unit tests for each of them. This promotes testability and allows us to verify their functionality in isolation.

Step 5: Extensibility

Now, if we need to add new features or modify existing ones, we can do so without affecting the entire Employee class. This follows the Open-Closed Principle (OCP), as we can extend the system without modifying existing code.

Step 6: Maintainability

By adhering to clean code principles and creating well-structured classes, we improve the maintainability of our codebase. Developers can work on individual classes without causing unintended side effects in other parts of the system.

Step 7: Better Separation of Concerns

The restructuring provides a clear separation of concerns. EmployeeInfo focuses on employee data, while BonusCalculator handles bonus calculations. This makes the codebase more organized and easier to understand.

In conclusion, restructuring the Employee class into smaller, focused classes enhances code quality, maintainability, and extensibility. It aligns with clean code principles and sets the stage for a more robust and adaptable system.

Section 20.4: The Final Transformed Employee

After the restructuring process discussed in the previous section, we have successfully transformed the Employee class into a more maintainable and organized structure. In this section, we'll examine the final version of the Employee class and discuss the benefits of this transformation.

The Transformed Employee Class

The final version of the Employee class is now composed of two distinct classes: EmployeeInfo and BonusCalculator. Let's briefly review each of these classes:

EmployeeInfo Class

The EmployeeInfo class is responsible for managing employee information, such as name, employee ID, and department. Here's a summarized version of the class:

```python
class EmployeeInfo:

def __init__(self, name, employee_id, department):

self.name = name

self.employee_id = employee_id

self.department = department
```

This class encapsulates all the attributes related to an employee's personal information.

BonusCalculator Class

The BonusCalculator class handles the logic for calculating bonuses based on specific criteria. Here's a simplified example:

class BonusCalculator:

@staticmethod

def calculate_bonus(employee_info):

 # Logic for bonus calculation based on employee_info

pass

This class is designed to calculate bonuses independently of the employee's personal information.

Benefits of the Transformation

The transformation of the Employee class into these two separate classes offers several advantages:

1. **Improved Readability:** The code is now more readable and comprehensible because it adheres to the Single Responsibility Principle (SRP). Each class has a clear and distinct purpose.
2. **Enhanced Testability:** With separate classes, it becomes easier to write unit tests for each component. You can test the EmployeeInfo class for correctness of personal information handling and the BonusCalculator class for accurate bonus calculations.

3. **Flexibility and Extensibility:** The codebase is now more flexible and extensible. If you need to add new features or modify bonus calculation rules, you can do so within the BonusCalculator class without affecting the EmployeeInfo class or other parts of the system. This aligns with the Open-Closed Principle (OCP).

4. **Reduced Coupling:** The separation of concerns and well-defined interfaces between classes results in reduced coupling. Changes in one class are less likely to affect others, which leads to a more stable codebase.

5. **Maintenance and Collaboration:** Developers can work on individual classes independently, making it easier to maintain and collaborate on the codebase. Each class has a clear purpose, reducing the risk of unintended side effects.

6. **Organized Codebase:** The codebase is now more organized, with classes focused on specific responsibilities. This enhances code clarity and makes it easier for developers to navigate and understand.

Conclusion

The transformation of the Employee class exemplifies the principles of clean code and object-oriented design. By separating responsibilities, adhering to SRP, and promoting flexibility and testability, we've created a more maintainable and adaptable codebase. This transformation serves as a valuable example of how clean code practices can lead to better software design and development.

Section 20.5: The Journey to Clean Code

In this final section of the book, we reflect on the journey we've taken towards writing clean code and the lessons we've learned along the way. The transformation of the Employee class that we discussed in the previous sections is just one example of how clean code principles can significantly impact software development. Let's summarize some key takeaways from our journey.

1. Principles of Clean Code

Throughout the book, we've explored fundamental principles of clean code, such as meaningful names, small and focused functions, single responsibility, and open-closed design. These principles serve as guidelines for writing code that is easy to understand, maintain, and extend.

2. Object-Oriented Design

Object-oriented design principles, like encapsulation, inheritance, and polymorphism, have played a crucial role in structuring our code effectively. By organizing code into classes and objects, we achieve modularity, reusability, and maintainability.

3. Test-Driven Development (TDD)

We've discussed the importance of unit testing and Test-Driven Development (TDD) in ensuring the reliability and correctness of our code. Writing tests before implementing functionality helps us catch bugs early and provides a safety net for refactoring.

4. Code Refactoring

Refactoring is an integral part of clean code development. It involves improving the structure and design of existing code without changing its external behavior. Through real-life examples like the refactoring of SerialDate, we've seen how refactoring can make code cleaner and more maintainable.

5. Design Patterns and Smells

Understanding design patterns and recognizing code smells are valuable skills for any developer. Design patterns provide proven solutions to common design problems, while recognizing code smells helps identify areas for improvement in existing code.

6. Continuous Improvement

Clean code is not a one-time effort; it's a mindset and a commitment to continuous improvement. By applying clean code practices consistently and seeking opportunities to refactor and enhance code quality, we can create software that stands the test of time.

7. Collaboration and Communication

Effective collaboration and communication among team members are essential for maintaining clean code. Code reviews, pair programming, and clear documentation help ensure that everyone is on the same page and that code adheres to established standards.

8. Software Craftsmanship

We've discussed the concept of software craftsmanship and the idea that writing code is not just a task but a craft. Taking pride in our work, striving for excellence, and continually honing our skills are key aspects of becoming better developers.

9. Flexibility and Adaptability

Clean code is not rigid; it's flexible and adaptable to changing requirements and circumstances. It allows us to respond to evolving needs without causing undue disruption or introducing unnecessary complexity.

10. The Clean Code Mindset

Above all, clean code is a mindset. It's a commitment to producing high-quality software that is easy to read, understand, and maintain. It's about taking ownership of our code and striving for excellence in everything we create.

As we conclude our journey through the world of clean code, remember that it's an ongoing process of growth and improvement. The principles and practices discussed in this book are tools in your developer's toolkit, and by using them wisely, you can create software that not only works but also shines. Embrace the clean code mindset, share your knowledge with others, and continue your quest to become a better developer.